JAPAN'S ECONOMIC ROLE IN NORTHEAST ASIA

The Asia Society is a nonprofit, nonpartisan public education organization dedicated to increasing American understanding of Asia and its growing importance to the United States and to world relations. Founded in 1956, the Society covers all of Asia—22 countries from Japan to Iran and from Soviet Central Asia to the South Pacific islands. Through its programs in contemporary affairs, the fine and performing arts, and elementary and secondary education, the Society reaches audiences across the United States and works closely with colleagues in Asia.

The *Asian Agenda* program of The Asia Society seeks to . . .

- Alert Americans to the key Asian issues of the 1980s

- Illuminate the policy choices facing decision-makers in the public and private sectors

- Strengthen the dialogue between Americans and Asians on the issues and their policy implications.

Asian Agenda issues are identified in consultation with a group of advisors and are addressed through studies and publications, national and international conferences, public programs around the U.S., and media activities. Major funding for the Asian Agenda program is currently provided by the Ford Foundation, the Rockefeller Foundation, the Andrew W. Mellon Foundation, the Henry Luce Foundation, the Rockefeller Brothers Fund, and the United States-Japan Foundation.

JAPAN'S ECONOMIC ROLE IN NORTHEAST ASIA

by Edward J. Lincoln

UNIVERSITY PRESS OF AMERICA

LANHAM • NEW YORK • LONDON

Co-published by arrangement with
The Asia Society,
725 Park Avenue, New York, New York 10021

Library of Congress Cataloging in Publication Data

Lincoln, Edward J.
  Japan's economic role in Northeast Asia.

  (Asian agenda report ; 10)
    1. Japan—Foreign economic relations—East Asia.
  2. East Asia—Foreign economic relations—Japan.
  3. Japan—Economic conditions—1868-   . 4. East
  Asia—Economic conditions.   5. Investments, American—
  East Asia.   I. Title.   II. Series.
  HF1602.15.E2L55   1986   337.5205   86-22439
  ISBN 0-8191-5677-9 (alk. paper)
  ISBN 0-8191-5678-7 (pbk. : alk. paper)

Contents

List of Tables

SOVIET UNION

Soviet
Kamchatka

Sea of Okhotsk

Kurile Islands

Soviet
Sakhalin

Administered by
Soviet Union
claimed by Japan

Vladivostok

Sea of
Japan

NORTH
KOREA

Tokyo

MONGOLIA

Ulan Bator

P'yongyang

Demarcation Line,
July 27, 1953

JAPAN

Beijing

Seoul
SOUTH
KOREA

Korea Strait

Yellow
Sea

CHINA

East
China
Sea

Taipei

Hong Kong

TAIWAN

Macao

Northeast Asia

Foreword

In the years ahead Japan and the United States will face challenges to their interests and to their partnership in the Asian regional setting. How the two nations respond to changing conditions in the region will have significant consequences for other nations as well. The challenge is especially evident in Northeast Asia, where vital security interests of both nations are at stake and where economic relations are changing rapidly.

The Soviet military buildup in Northeast Asia, the confrontations on the Korean peninsula, the evolution of the Sino-Soviet relationship, and the Taiwan question make the security situation in the region one of the most sensitive and complex in the world. Political and security relations are further complicated by historic economic developments such as the opening and reform of China's economy, the emergence of Korea and Taiwan as major trading nations and competitors with Japan in some sectors, and the mounting pressure on Japan to reorient its economy. While most Americans and Japanese are focusing their attention on strains in their bilateral relationship, the potential for cooperation and conflict arising from these trends and issues has received relatively little notice. But successful management of U.S.-Japan interactions in Northeast Asia will require wider understanding in both countries.

This report is one result of a multiyear project sponsored by The Asia Society that seeks to stimulate greater American attention to U.S.-Japan interactions in Asia. The first phase of the project on "Japan, the United States and a Changing Asia" focused on Japanese and American interests and roles in Southeast Asia. It included an international conference in Japan in July 1984 that brought together more than fifty Americans, Japanese and Southeast Asians, a report authored by Charles Morrison of the East-West Center and published in the Asian Agenda report series, and a series of regional programs held in seven U.S. cities in February 1985.

The second phase of the project has examined the multilateral relations of Japan and the United States in Northeast Asia and has sought to stimulate wider discussion of them between Americans and Japanese and in the United States. In the fall of 1985 The Asia Society organized two study missions. The first, consisting of seven American specialists on Asian affairs, visited seven political and financial capitals of Northeast Asia to obtain the views of government officials, scholars, business people, educators and journalists on the international relations of the region. A second study team consisting of fifteen leaders from across the

United States drawn from several professional fields visited Japan for a week of briefings and discussions with Japanese officials, scholars and journalists on Northeast Asian affairs. A conference in Japan in November 1985 brought the two American teams together with Japanese counterparts for an exchange of views on the region.

This process of international dialogue provided the basis for an array of education outreach activities in the United States. These included lectures by the American specialists in different parts of the United States during the winter and spring of 1986, miniconferences in six American cities during May 1986 in which the American specialists and visiting Asian scholars discussed the region before diverse audiences, and a series of monographs by the American specialists on key topics relating to Japan and the United States in Northeast Asia. These monographs, including the present volume, are being published separately by The Asia Society in its Asian Agenda report series for wide distribution around the United States and Asia.

The specialist study mission was led by Professor Robert A. Scalapino of the University of California at Berkeley, one of the United States' leading authorities on Asian affairs. The other members included distinguished scholars representing different disciplines and area specialties: Herbert Ellison, an historian of Russia and the Soviet Union who was then director of the Kennan Institute of Advanced Russian Studies in Washington, D.C. and is now at the University of Washington, Seattle; Harry Harding, a political scientist specializing on China and Senior Fellow at the Brookings Institution; Donald Hellmann, a scholar of Japanese politics and foreign policy at the University of Washington, Seattle; Nicholas Lardy, a specialist on the Chinese economy also at the University of Washington, Seattle; Edward J. Lincoln, an economist working on Japan at the Brookings Institution; and myself (Marshall M. Bouton), representing The Asia Society.

Over a period of five weeks in October–November 1985 the Northeast Asian study mission visited Tokyo, Moscow, Ulan Bator, Beijing, Hong Kong, Taipei and Seoul. The mission also sought to visit Pyongyang but was not granted permission to do so by the North Korean authorities. In the course of its mission the American team met with over two hundred and fifty officials, scholars, journalists and business people. This intensive schedule of discussions was made possible through the generous assistance of host organizations in all seven cities: the Japan Center for International Exchange in Tokyo; the Institute of Oriental Studies in Moscow; the Executive Committee of the Union of Mongolian Organizations for Peace and Friendship with Other Countries in Ulan Bator; the Chinese Academy of Social Sciences in Beijing; the Universities Service Center in Hong Kong; the Institute of International Relations in Taipei; and the Asiatic Research Center of Korea

University in Seoul. The Asia Society is deeply grateful for this assistance.

This report is the latest in a series produced by The Asia Society's national public education program on contemporary Asian affairs, "America's Asian Agenda". The Asian Agenda program seeks to alert Americans to critical issues in Asian affairs and in U.S.-Asia relations, to illuminate the choices which public and private policy-makers face, and to strengthen trans-Pacific dialogue on the issues. Through studies, national and international conferences, regional public programs in the United States, and corporate and media activities, the program involves American and Asian specialists and opinion-leaders in a far-reaching educational process. Asian Agenda publications emphasize short, timely reports aimed at a wide readership. Other recently published and forthcoming Asian Agenda reports address a variety of topics including Christianity in contemporary Korea, the United States and the ANZUS alliance, financing Asian growth and development, and the Philippines and the United States.

The Asia Society wishes to acknowledge the roles played by a number of individuals and organizations in the activities leading to this report. First, the Society is deeply indebted to Robert A. Scalapino for his extraordinary leadership of the American specialist mission to Northeast Asia. His exceptional knowledge, energy and goodwill were essential to the success of a complex and demanding endeavor. The Society is equally grateful to the other distinguished team members for their valuable contributions to the mission and other components of the project. Special thanks are also due to the leaders of the Asian organizations that arranged our programs: Tadashi Yamamoto, Evgenii Primakov, Luvsanchultem, Zhao Fusan, John Dolfin, Yu-Ming Shaw and Han Sung-Joo. We wish also to express deep appreciation to the many individuals in the cities visited who took time from their very busy schedules to talk with the team at length.

Major financial support for the project on "Japan, the United States and a Changing Northeast Asia" has been generously provided by the United States-Japan Foundation. The Japan-United States Friendship Commission made available monies for the U.S. regional programming of the project. Critical also was funding provided for the Society's Asian Agenda program by the Ford, Rockefeller and Henry Luce foundations and the Rockefeller Brothers Fund.

Finally, several members of the Society's staff were instrumental in the development of the project and the publications. John Bresnan assisted in the project's original overall design. Ernest Notar played an important early role in the project's phase on Northeast Asia. Most central to that second phase were Timothy J.C. O'Shea, who very ably organized all the project's activities, and Rose Wright, who provided excellent administrative assistance. Eileen D. Chang skillfully guided the publication of this and other reports emerging from the project.

Marshall M. Bouton
Director, Contemporary Affairs
The Asia Society
June, 1986

Preface

If one had to choose a single region of greatest importance to Americans in terms of their livelihood, political values and security, a leading candidate would be Northeast Asia. It is here that the most intensive economic interaction involving the United States will take place in the years immediately ahead, with interdependence — and the problems attendant to it — steadily advancing. It is here that the capacities of diverse societies to achieve and maintain a greater degree of political openness will be tested. And it is here that global and regional security issues are inextricably connected, with fateful consequences for all mankind.

In considering the future of Northeast Asia, one must juxtapose two equally important factors. On the one hand, each of the nation-states within the region bears a primary responsibility for the welfare of its own people, and the strength of its domestic political and social fabric. The decisions made by the leaders of each society are especially crucial at a time when virtually every government stands at a crossroads, facing the necessity of reconsidering past economic policies, political institutions and security strategies. Any attempt to shift the principal responsibility to external forces is fallacious.

At the same time, two nations — the United States and Japan — are deeply interrelated with both the developmental and security issues that confront the region as a whole. In their very dynamism, and the extraordinary reach of their power — economic, political or military — they cannot avoid exerting a major influence throughout Northeast Asia. Inaction as well as action sends its message, creates an impact. Their domestic policies no less than their foreign policies have far-reaching repercussions.

It thus seemed important and timely to undertake a study on United States and Japanese policies in a changing Northeast Asia. In liaison with knowledgeable Japanese, we set about examining our respective roles in the region — past, present and future.

Our task was to draw upon our background as students of Asia, supplementing this with a journey to all parts of the region available to us to hear the current ideas and proposals of Asians representing various political, economic and national perspectives. During the course of our five-week trip, we sought first to discern those indigenous elements of a geopolitical, ideological or economic nature that helped to shape a given society's attitudes and policies toward its neighbors, toward the region as a whole and especially toward the United States and Japan. We also explored the issues of greatest concern to our respondents and their views as to the appropriate remedial action. At various points, attention focused upon the question of American and Japanese policies, with an effort to examine viable alternatives as well as the potentials that existed in current policies.

On occasion, as individuals we held different views from our Asian or Soviet friends, either with respect to the relevant data or the conclusions to be drawn from it. Being Americans, moreover, we sometimes differed among ourselves. The monograph that follows, and the others in this series, thus represent the views of the author. No effort has been made to achieve a complete consensus among us. Nevertheless, those who read all of the monographs will discover a very considerable measure of agreement on most matters of consequence.

We are enormously grateful to those individuals and organizations throughout Northeast Asia and in the Soviet Union who served as hosts, facilitators, and discussants. To exchange views in a concentrated fashion, and to have the opportunity to compare and contrast the views in one society with those in another over a very short period of time proved both enlightening and stimulating.

On behalf of the group, let me also express our deep gratitude to The Asia Society and its principal officers, especially Marshall Bouton, for making possible an experience that was both enriching and enjoyable.

Robert A. Scalapino
Berkeley, California

Executive Summary

Because Japan has played a relatively limited role in international diplomacy in the postwar period, Americans tend to forget that it plays an enormously important economic role in Northeast Asia. In many respects, Japan has truly become an economic giant; it is an advanced industrial power with the second largest economy in the world. Since Japan sits on the edge of Northeast Asia, it quite naturally plays an important role in the region. Economic growth in Northeast Asia has been very high, and although Japan's economic role has been a positive factor, the situation contains some serious problems.

The purpose of this monograph is to introduce Americans to the basic elements of Japan's economic relationships in this diverse and important region of the world. The discussion begins with Japan itself: its emergence as a mature industrial colossus and the changes that maturity has brought. This is followed by a review of U.S.-Japan relations, the most important bilateral economic tie in the region and the starting point for understanding the others. Finally, because of their extreme diversity in terms of both economic development and political systems, the other Northeast Asian countries are divided into three groups for analysis: the newly industrializing market economies (South Korea, Taiwan and Hong Kong), a developing socialist economy (China) and the Soviet bloc (Mongolia, North Korea and the Soviet Union). Although some general features pertain to Japan's relations with all of these countries, there are a number of striking differences that account for this division.

Japan's Emergence

Japan's rise to join the ranks of advanced industrial countries in the twentieth century has been one of the outstanding shifts in the world economic scene. Beginning in the second half of the nineteenth century, Japan had made considerable progress along this route prior to the war, but the real miracle came in the postwar period. Bolstered by a strong education system, an aggressive private-sector and a supportive government, Japan was able to efficiently import and adapt foreign technology to Japanese conditions. The average 10 percent real growth of the economy from the 1950s until the early 1970s was the highest in the world.

Many Americans are now aware of the high growth of the Japanese economy. Far fewer, though, realize that this era came to a crashing halt in 1974, after which growth has been much more modest. While Japan has on average continued to grow somewhat faster than the United States, the disparity has not been as wide as before. Japan's more moderate performance is mainly the result of its success; by the 1970s Japan had largely caught up with the United States and the other industrial countries, limiting the possibility of further rapid gains from imports of advanced technology.

This important downward shift in growth has brought important changes in the economy's macroeconomic balances that are key to understanding Japan's economic ties with Northeast Asia. During the high-growth era, Japan had provided the necessary investment resources for expansion from its high domestic savings, eliminating the need for heavy borrowing from abroad. However, when the growth rate dropped, the society continued to generate high levels of savings that were no longer matched by strong private-sector investment. That excess of savings over investment in the private sector had to be absorbed elsewhere in the economic system. In Japan, it went to both a rapidly increasing government fiscal deficit and a current-account surplus with the rest of the world. In the 1980s, the international surpluses became larger as the government carried out austerity policies to reduce its fiscal deficits. Within the context of global current-account surpluses, Japan has had trade surpluses with all of the countries in Northeast Asia.This fact has soured Japan's regional economic relations.

Further damaging Japan's international reputation has been the incomplete dismantling of the strong barriers against imports and inward investment that characterized Japan in the early postwar years. Lacking a strong domestic constituency for free trade, the process of liberalization has required heavy pressure from the United States and other trading partners, and this pattern shows little change. As Japan's surpluses mounted in the 1980s, international criticism has become stronger because of a belief that surplus countries ought to be the leaders of the international liberal trade system.

The U.S.-Japan Relationship

During the first half of the 1980s the U.S. economy moved in exactly the opposite direction as Japan. The very large government deficits brought about by the Reagan administration's fiscal policies, combined with private-sector demand for investment funds, exceeded the supply of savings available in the economy. This pushed the United States into a large global current-account and trade deficit, including an enormous increase in its bilateral deficit with Japan, which reached $46 billion in 1985. This deterioration contributed to the increasingly tense tone of bilateral discussions. While no large-scale protectionist action directed against Japan has emerged from Congress, the trend toward harsh criticism and threats of retaliation is very serious.

Several features of the U.S.-Japan bilateral relationship are important for the rest of Northeast Asia. First, the depth of the frustration with Japan evident in Washington is striking and could spill over into U.S. relations with other countries in the region, as many in those countries believe it already has. Second, the United States appears to have carried most of the burden of negotiating with Japan. Third, not until 1986 were Japan and the United States willing to consider changes in their respective macroeconomic policies that had led to the combination of large U.S. trade deficits and Japanese trade surpluses.

Northeast Asia

Looking at the rest of Northeast Asia, Japan's economic role is important and growing, but unbalanced. Whereas Japan is the largest single source of imports for most of these countries, it is not the largest single export destination for any of them. This fact has been a primary element in the criticism of Japan in the region. Another feature revealed by the trade data is that Japan has not replaced the United States as a dominant economic actor in the region. Japan and the United States share the role as the largest trading partners for these countries, and the position of the United States has not been substantially reduced in the past decade.

In addition to international trade, Japan is tied to the region by capital flows, foreign aid and technology flows. All of these point to a strong, positive role for Japan. For direct foreign investment, Japan again shares with the United States the role of largest investor in these countries. For foreign aid, Japan is now the dominant supplier, though only South Korea and China are eligible recipients among the nations of the region. And as for technology flows, Japan has emerged as an important technology exporter as it has approached the world technological frontier. However, all of these ties have involved some controversy and criticism of Japan for stinginess or actions that would seem to benefit Japanese industry more than the recipient countries.

The Newly Industrializing Countries (NICs)

Although they are separated considerably by income levels and development strategy, South Korea, Taiwan and Hong Kong form a convenient subdivision of Northeast Asia as they have a number of elements in common. These are the countries in the region with the highest growth performance over the past decade. In assessing their relationship with Japan, however, several features stand out.

First, these are economies highly dependent on trade for the growth and development of their domestic economies. With ratios of exports to gross national product (GNP) that range from 35 to 89 percent, the economic performances of these countries are highly dependent on trends in world trade. In addition, their major export markets tend to be

xvii

the United States and Japan. Changes in U.S. and Japanese economic growth as well as U.S.-Japan trade tensions are of great importance to them.

Second, all face uncertainties in their economic future beyond their dependence on these two large countries. These countries are incomplete democracies that face future political uncertainties. South Korea also lives under the cloud of potential conflict with North Korea; Taiwan faces an unknown future relationship with China; and Hong Kong reverts to Chinese ownership in 1997, with no clear ideas of what that will mean. These uncertainties suggest that a shift in Japan's economic ties away from the United States and toward these countries is unlikely.

Third, Japan is important to these three countries through the variety of economic ties mentioned above, but these relationships are somewhat weaker than one might expect given geographic proximity and some common elements of Sinitic culture. Japan outdistances the United States as a supplier of goods to these countries by only a small margin (except for Hong Kong), and on the export side the United States absorbs a far greater share than does Japan. In addition, Japan's relative role has actually diminished over time, as the trade ties of these countries have shifted more toward the United States and the rest of the world.

Finally, none of these countries are currently expressing the level of frustration with Japan that typifies reactions in Washington. Whereas they have complained often in the past, the current mood is relatively restrained. In fact, more criticism is being directed at Washington than at Tokyo.

China

China forms another subdivision of Northeast Asia. It is a socialist country that has recently undergone extensive reforms that have brought it back into extensive economic interaction with the capitalist world. In the space of just a few years since the major reforms began in 1978, Japan has forged a strong economic relationship with China, encompassing trade, direct investment, loans, foreign aid and technology transfer. The trade ties, in fact, are stronger than those of the NICs with Japan. These ties have contributed to China's development goals and have made the two nations relatively satisfied with their bilateral relationship despite Chinese complaints about various aspects of it.

The strength and relative smoothness of this relationship does not imply the coming of a China-Japan economic combination that will dominate regional or world markets. The enthusiasm of the Japanese for China is tempered by caution about the incomplete institutional framework for international business in China, the unpredictability of Chinese policy and concern that China could become a future competitor. The Chinese, on the other hand, appear to desire a balance among their foreign economic partners and will use their strong control over trade and investment to prevent Japan from becoming too dominant.

China also faces a serious constraint in its trade with Japan. The bulk of Chinese exports to Japan are raw materials. Low economic growth in Japan is limiting the demand for raw materials, and falling prices are decreasing their value. Because imports from Japan are necessary to fuel industrial development, China must develop manufactured exports to compensate for the drop in raw material exports if it is to avoid a large bilateral trade deficit. China may also periodically clamp down on its imports from Japan to control the imbalance.

The Soviet Bloc

After looking at the large role that Japan plays in the external ties of all other nations of Northeast Asia, the very limited relationships with the Soviet Union and its two close allies in the region are very striking. Japan's economic ties with both Mongolia and North Korea are so miniscule that they are virtually nonexistent at the present time. With the Soviet Union the ties are stronger but represent minor shares in both country's total trade. In addition, the level of Japan-Soviet trade dropped substantially in the first half of the 1980s.

Soviet ideology has dominated the relationship. Soviet officials seem to have some difficulty accepting Japan as a mature, technologically advanced nation. In addition, they display considerable contempt for Japan's close economic and strategic relationship with the United States.

The contempt and lack of interest in Japan, however, may be misleading, and as Mr. Gorbachev establishes his agenda, a more active Soviet Union is likely to try to improve its economic and political position in Northeast Asia. Yet, any dramatic improvement in economic ties with Japan is highly unlikely. First, even a considerable growth in trade would only return the situation to where it was at the beginning of the 1980s. Second, the Soviets face the same problem of dependency on raw material exports to Japan as does China and may face greater difficulties in moving away from that dependency. Third, the Japanese have become more wary of the Soviet Union over the past decade as the result of a long series of Soviet provocations and incidents. An upturn in world prices of the raw materials that the Soviet Union exports to Japan or a willingness to make Japanese participation in investment projects in the Soviet Union more profitable could change this picture, but neither of these eventualities appears likely at the present time.

Conclusion

Japan's economic impact on the countries of Northeast Asia is quite large in all cases except the Soviet bloc. Economists view international economic ties through trade, investment and technology as beneficial because they allow the scarce economic resources of the world to be put to the most productive use to the mutual benefit of all countries concerned. Japan's rapid industrialization and growing ties within the region have helped that process take place. Nonetheless, the purely economic gains from this relationship have been accompanied by a number of serious political problems.

From an American perspective, Japan has been increasingly viewed as an economic threat or as unfair in its trading practices, a development exacerbated by the large global and bilateral trade imbalances of the 1980s. This has raised the specter of a serious retreat from the liberal international trade and investment regime that has characterized the postwar period.

If the nations of Northeast Asia are to continue to grow and develop, then Japan must deal with two critical issues. First, it must be willing to adopt macroeconomic policies that will shift its own growth away from dependence on exports toward domestic demand. The large Japanese trade surpluses and U.S. trade deficits that emerged in the first half of the 1980s are not sustainable either economically or politically in the long run. Both Japan and the United States must address this problem and continue the progress that began with the efforts to alter exchange rates in the fall of 1985.

Second, Japan must continue to lower barriers to its markets in order to contain criticism from abroad. Should Japan fail to do so, the result could well be a serious protectionist outburst by the United States which would necessarily spill over to the countries of the region. Both Japan and the United States bear the responsibility for managing their bilateral relationship, but the critical element will be Japan's willingness to continue the progress toward liberal trade.

If Japan, in conjunction with the United States, can appropriately manage its macroeconomic and trade policies, then the prospects for the region remain promising. But success in dealing with these problems is far from assured.

I. Introduction

Because Japan has played a relatively limited role in international diplomacy in the postwar period, Americans tend to forget that it plays an enormously important economic role in Northeast Asia. Focusing on our own ties with individual Asian countries, it is easy to lose sight of the fact that their economic connections with Japan are often equally close. In many respects, Japan has truly become an economic giant; it is an advanced industrial power with the second largest economy in the world. Since Japan sits on the edge of Northeast Asia, it quite naturally plays an important role in the region.

People tend to shy away from economic issues because they seem too complex, too mathematical or less exciting than political and military developments. However, economics need not be discussed in arcane language, and it most certainly should not be ignored. Many of the important political and strategic developments in Northeast Asia are strongly affected by economic factors, and Japan is a key element in many of these developments. If we wish to understand the region better and implement intelligent policies, then we must understand the economic side of these issues.

This broad topic has many dimensions because the economies of Northeast Asia are extremely diverse. In terms of income levels, the range is from two of the richest countries in the world (the United States and Japan) to one of the poorest (China). Economic systems also differ, with the region including both capitalist and socialist economies, and with wide variations in the economic role of the government within both of those broad types.

The purpose of this monograph is to introduce Americans to the basic elements of Japan's economic relationships in this diverse and important region of the world. The discussion begins with a consideration of Japan itself: its emergence as a mature industrial colossus and the changes that maturity has brought. This is followed by a review of U.S.-Japan relations, the most important bilateral economic tie in the region and the starting point for understanding the others. Finally, because of their diversity, the other Northeast Asian countries are divided into three groups for analysis: the newly industrializing market economies (South Korea, Taiwan and Hong Kong), a developing socialist economy (China), and the Soviet bloc (Mongolia, North Korea and the Soviet Union). Although some general features pertain to Japan's relations with all of these countries, there are a number of striking differences that lead to this division.

1

The discussion in the following pages emphasizes three general propositions about Japan's economic role in Northeast Asia. First, that role is of great importance and should not be ignored, but it has not led to any serious erosion of the U.S. economic role in the region. Second, the nature of this interaction is to everyone's *economic* benefit. The United States and the countries of the region are economically better off with a rich Japan than they were with a poor Japan. Third, such generally optimistic conclusions do need to be tempered by recognition of a series of problems, including the continuation of Japan's large current-account surpluses, potential disruption from U.S.-Japan trade conflicts, potential obstacles elsewhere in the region to Japan's continued rapid growth, and the lack of truly international attitudes or policies in Japan. All of these points will be explored in greater detail later.

Optimism may seem unjustified. All too often in the United States, people see Japan in terms of an economic threat: imports are viewed as destroying jobs in American industries; Japan is described as capturing markets in other Asian countries once dominated by the United States; and sometimes Japan is even seen as winning through economic dominance what it lost in the Second World War. Although these stereotypes may be superficially appealing, they bear little resemblance to reality, and a major purpose of this monograph is to explain why.

Some Basic Concepts

Economic theory deals with a simple but central problem: the wants or desires of individuals are boundless, while the resources available to satisfy those desires are limited. The fundamental question addressed by economic theory is how to allocate goods or resources in a way that maximizes satisfaction. This problem can be stated in two ways. First, at any particular time, what allocation of resources is the most efficient in the sense of producing the largest amount of goods in the proportions desired by society? Second, over time, what choices about consumption versus investment or about the allocation of investment resources provide maximum satisfaction? Each of these basic questions raises a host of others: What kinds of economic organizations bring about the most efficient allocation? What kinds of government policies are the most appropriate in reaching the goal of the most efficient allocation? What kinds of problems can arise that prevent an economic system from operating efficiently? The list is endless. Economists may not be very good at providing clear answers to all of these questions, but they do provide a method of analyzing them that can be very useful.

Economists disagree on many issues, yet most would agree with the following simple but important statements:

1. Economic transactions are generally not zero-sum. Individuals and corporations make decisions that benefit themselves, given their income constraints and the price of goods and services in the marketplace. In a larger context, choices that lead to the movement of resources from one part of the economy to another may leave particular individuals or corporations worse off, but if the reallocation is economically efficient, the losers can be compensated. Such reallocations of resources within an economy (such as the movement of the U.S. textile industry from New England to the South earlier in this century) may also impose short-term adjustment costs as people shift to other jobs or even other geographical locations, but economists generally believe that long-term gains in efficiency far outweigh these adjustment costs.

2. On an international scale, positive-sum transactions include the concept of comparative advantage. Nations are better off with international trade than without it. By engaging in trade, each nation can shift its own resources toward production of those products in which it has a comparative advantage. One nation can be less efficient than another in all areas of production and still benefit from trade; it will produce and export those products in which its relative disadvantage is the least and import those in which its disadvantage is the greatest. The notion that unrestricted foreign competition would drive all American companies out of business because of low foreign wages, for example, is entirely unfounded. Lower wages are an advantage for products with a relatively high labor content. Even with Japan, a country with high wages, unrestricted bilateral trade is to our mutual benefit, with Japan and the United States each exporting products in which it has a relative advantage. This concept is widely accepted among economists and lies behind the movement over the past forty years to lower trade barriers around the world.

3. Competition helps to drive economic systems toward an efficient allocation of resources. In capitalist systems, competition among profit-seeking firms leads to the success of the most efficient and the failure of the inefficient. In socialist systems the challenge is to provide a functional equivalent of competition without the existence of private ownership and private distribution of the profits or rewards from efficiency. No capitalist or socialist system works perfectly, and there are many examples where competition does not lead to the desired result, but the general proposition that competition is desirable remains true. Most people accept this abstract concept but have trouble accepting the consequences: inefficiency loses in competition.

4. Everything that is produced by an economic system must be accounted for. The concept behind this statement forms a large part of macroeconomics. In a given country, if people choose to save part of

their income, those savings must be used elsewhere in the economic system, either in the private sector, in government or abroad. If the amount saved does not equal the amount borrowed, then the economy must adjust to bring the two into equality.

In an international setting, the same principle applies: What leaves the country will necessarily equal what enters the country. The accounting framework for a country's international transactions is called the balance of payments, and the bottom line must be zero. Within the balance of payments there are a number of subdivisions; most often mentioned is the current account, consisting of merchandise trade, services, and transfers (that is, foreign aid). The sum of all accounts in the balance of payments — though not necessarily of any of its subdivisions — will be zero. If a country has a surplus on its current account, then it will by definition have a deficit on capital flows (that is, net acquisition of foreign financial assets).

Economics is an extremely complex subject, but much of the theory can be reduced to a few elementary points like these four. Although they all seem obvious, it is surprising how much of the public discussion of international economic issues completely ignores them. We see competition with other countries in a zero-sum context; we fear that foreigners will destroy the economic fabric of the United States through trade; we deny that competition is desirable when it crosses national boundaries; and we fail to acknowledge the macroeconomic balances that are a fundamental part of international economic flows.

II. The Economic Background

Japan's economic relations with the region cannot be understood without some knowledge of Japan itself. Several features of the country are reviewed in this section, including Japan's emergence as an advanced industrial country, the macroeconomic implications of its economic maturity, and its approach to foreign economic policy. Each raises issues that are important to Japan's relations with other countries in Northeast Asia. In brief, Japan's economic growth and development has been of great benefit to the region, but slower growth has pushed the country into large current-account surpluses (and capital outflows) that have become a major problem for its trading partners. It has responded with a grudging, piecemeal lowering of the import barriers that have so severely hurt its international reputation.

Japan's Emergence as an Industrial Nation

A fundamental shift in the world economic scene in the twentieth century has been the rise of Japan to join the ranks of advanced industrial countries. Forced to open to world trade in the mid-nineteenth century, Japan soon experienced a revolution that created a nation-state. The leaders of the new central government quickly decided that adopting Western technology was the only feasible way to fend off the imperialist challenge. To avoid suffering a fate similar to that of Southeast Asia or China, Japan's leaders worked to provide a modern institutional framework that would be supportive of economic development, and they encouraged the private sector in a variety of ways.

By the beginning of the twentieth century, that framework had been established and businessmen were actively applying foreign technology to create a modern industrial base. Through a combination of hard work, import and adaptation of foreign technology, a strong educational program, a reasonably stable domestic political situation, and a certain amount of luck, Japan's economy grew faster than that of the United States or European countries in the first two decades of the century. By the 1920s, it was beginning to be a significant factor in such world markets as textiles.

The 1930s brought a descent into nightmare for Japan, but business continued to grow and prosper until the destruction of war finally hit the home islands. The devastation left Japan unable even to feed its population in 1945 without aid from the United States. With the major industrial cities reduced to rubble, inflation rampant, severe scarcity of even

5

daily necessities, and the return of five to nine million people from overseas possessions and the military, Japan set about rebuilding itself.

Out of those ashes, Japan has achieved a miraculous resurgence. What economists call real growth (that is, growth after subtracting inflation) averaged 10 percent from 1950–1973, the highest sustained level of growth in the world. A number of factors propelled this expansion. Japan lagged far behind many other countries in technology at the beginning of the postwar period because its prewar development had been incomplete and because it had been relatively isolated from foreign technological trends from the late 1930s until the early 1950s. But a strong education system, aggressive corporate policies and a supportive government enabled it to import and adapt this technology to Japanese needs. Foreign companies were often willing to sell or license technologies and products to Japanese firms for three reasons: stringent trade barriers prevented the foreign companies from directly selling their products in Japan; investment barriers often precluded them from putting their own factories there; and they did not see the small and relatively backward Japanese companies as a potential competitive threat.

The willingness of Japanese companies to invest heavily in production based on new, borrowed technologies was enhanced by a large pool of available labor. Forced back onto the family farm by the destruction of the war, many Japanese were eager to work in industry as jobs became available without driving up wages. Since increased output was based on the more productive technologies borrowed from abroad, this pool of labor implied that productivity tended to rise more rapidly than wages during the 1950s and 1960s, with the difference appearing as increased corporate profits. This pattern differed from what economists expect in mature economies, where high growth puts pressure on labor markets and drives up wages faster than productivity, which then generates a downturn in growth.

High corporate profits in Japan resulting from investment in new technologies simply encouraged the investment process to continue. The government supported the process in a variety of ways, but principally through erecting very high trade barriers and creating a domestic economic environment favorable to business. Great controversy surrounds the question of the impact of government policy on Japan's economic performance. Many policies were foolish or of marginal importance, but the net impact of all government policies was undoubtedly favorable.

Another of the economic principles discussed in the introduction comes into play in this explanation of high growth: Since everything in the economy must be accounted for, the very high levels of investment in the private sector had to be matched by either high levels of domestic savings or an inflow of capital from abroad to provide the necessary funds. Many developing countries have chosen to borrow heavily from abroad to support their domestic investment; Japan did not. Fearful that large capital flows would undermine its ability to maintain a fixed exchange rate (and thereby damage its international credibility in the Bretton Woods exchange rate system that existed at that time), Japan imposed severe limitations on international capital flows, which essentially limited Japanese companies to domestic sources of funds. Therefore, the fact that Japan was able to invest at a high rate implies that the economy was also generating high levels of savings. All indicators show that from rather modest levels in the very early postwar period, savings rose at a rapid pace. By the 1960s, total private-sector savings in the economy were over 30 percent of GNP, a level about twice that of the United States.

Other factors also contributed to the very high growth of the Japanese economy. For example, most raw materials were characterized by declining or stable world prices at a time when Japan outstripped its own small resource base and became a major buyer on world markets. The postwar efforts to lower world trade barriers benefited Japanese exports, and exports had to grow in order to pay for both raw materials and the important inflow of foreign technology. Japan benefited from an extremely stable political system with smoothly functioning democratic institutions so that business profits and investment were not hurt by the periodic violence or repression that plague so many developing countries. Beyond these factors, growth was aided by Occupation reforms, early postwar aid from the United States, a broad public consensus on growth as a national goal, and other factors.

Many Americans are now aware of the high growth of the Japanese economy in the 1950s and 1960s. Far fewer, though, realize that this era came to a crashing halt in 1974, after which growth has been much more modest. This change was largely due to the success of high growth: by 1973 Japan had closed the technology gap that had allowed rapid jumps in productivity, and labor was no longer in plentiful supply. Efforts to promote rapid growth began to generate higher inflation rather than high real growth. To this basic shift can be added other factors that have acted to slow economic growth: social priorities shifted in the early 1970s from generating maximum growth to controlling pollution and providing better public amenities (such as parks, sidewalks and sewers); the oil shocks of 1973 and 1979 had a negative short-term impact and brought an expensive longer-term reallocation of resources away from energy-intensive industries; and the aging of the population has directed resources away from production to services for the elderly. All of these factors were becoming important at the beginning of the 1970s, but the oil shock of 1973 made for a dramatic break between eras of high and low growth.

7

Table 1
Real Growth of Gross National Product

	1960–1973	1974–1983
United States	4.0%	2.0%
Japan	10.6	3.7
West Germany	5.2	1.6
France (GDP)	5.7	2.3
Great Britain (GDP)	3.3	1.0
South Korea (GDP)	8.9	7.5
Hong Kong	7.9[a]	9.3
Taiwan	10.1	7.5
China	7.4[a]	6.0
Soviet Union	5.2[b]	3.0[b]

[a] Data for Hong Kong and China are taken from the *World Development Report, 1985,* and cover the years 1965–1973.
[b] Data for the Soviet Union are for 1961–1970 and 1971–1984.
Sources: IMF, *International Financial Statistics Yearbook,* 1985; World Bank, *World Development Report,* 1985; Council for Economic Planning and Development, Republic of China, *Taiwan Statistical Data Book,* 1985; and Central Intelligence Agency, *Handbook of Economic Statistics,* 1985.

Table 1 summarizes Japan's situation relative to other countries. During the 1950s and 1960s, Japan's growth rate, almost three times higher than that of the United States, far outdistanced European countries (even Germany), and by a smaller margin surpassed the countries that are currently considered to be high-growth. During the years from 1960 to 1973, Japan grew at the astounding average rate of 10.6 percent while the United States expanded at 4.0 percent. Taiwan came very close to Japan's performance, with 10.1 percent, but other Asian countries grew at rates well below 10 percent.

All industrial countries have grown more slowly since the oil shock of 1973, but Japan's real economic growth rate has dropped more than the others. From its record of growing almost three times as fast as the United States during the 1960s, Japan dropped to less than twice as fast. Over the past decade, U.S. growth has even surpassed that of Japan in several individual years. Although the Japanese growth rate has remained relatively good compared to other industrial countries, it has been weaker than it was earlier. Meanwhile, other developing countries have experienced far higher growth than Japan. Since they have not yet caught up with the industrial countries, their growth did not drop as much (and in the case of Hong Kong it even accelerated).

Forecasts of future economic growth in Japan anticipate a level not much different from the recent past. Economists agree on the expected slow growth of the labor force and capital stock, but there is less con-

8

sensus on the role of productivity change. The optimists see a revolution in microelectronics and new materials bringing about rapid productivity increases in the economy that will boost the overall rate of economic growth to five percent or above. The pessimists agree that technical change is continuing but are not convinced that it will bring about a large jump in the rate of productivity growth from what Japan has experienced in the past decade. Therefore, the current forecasts fall in a range of roughly 4–5 percent for average real GNP growth to the mid-1990s. I personally side with the pessimists: the revolution in microelectronics and other areas of technology is certainly reshaping our lives, but there is no reason to believe that the measured rate of productivity growth in Japan in the next decade will be higher than in the recent past. Whatever the outcome, Japan will continue to grow only moderately faster than the United States, and the gap in growth rates may turn out to be very small.

It may seem puzzling that Japan is growing rather slowly when its dominant image is one of enormously successful, rapidly expanding firms. Americans have become fascinated with Japanese management, product quality control, and the ability of Japanese firms to penetrate rapidly particular American markets. If these companies are so successful, why is Japan not growing faster than it is? The answer is twofold. First, we see only the most successful Japanese firms competing in the United States. Behind the facade of these aggressive companies is a country that is not yet as productive as the United States (though the gap is closing at a moderate rate). Second, even the successful firms in Japan are not growing as quickly as they were two decades ago. The large, diversified manufacturers that we see in the United States may be able to expand production and sales of particular new products at lightning speed, but in many cases their overall corporate growth and profit performance is not especially high.

The Macroeconomic Implications of Economic Maturity

The lower growth rate that has characterized Japan for the past decade and is likely to continue into the future has brought about important shifts in the economy's macroeconomic balances that are key to understanding Japan's economic ties with Northeast Asia. The changes are best explained by returning briefly to Japan's situation in its period of very rapid growth.

For a nation to grow, it must invest part of each year's output in expanded productive capacity. For the growth rate to be high, as it was in Japan, the proportion of output going to investment also must be high. Japan's high investment rate was supported not by funds borrowed from abroad but by domestic savings. As long as rapid growth continued, high levels of domestic savings were beneficial to Japan since

9

Table 2

Macroeconomic Balances in Japan

(as percentage shares of GNP)

	1970–1973	1974–1977	1978	1979	1980	1981	1982	1983
Private sector								
Savings	32.2%	30.6%	30.7%	29.0%	29.1%	28.5%	27.5%	27.2%
Investment	31.3	28.0	24.2	25.6	25.4	24.4	23.5	22.0
Balance	0.9	2.6	6.5	3.4	3.7	4.1	4.0	5.2
Government balance	0.9	(2.6)	(5.5)	(4.8)	(4.5)	(4.0)	(3.6)	(3.5)
Current account	1.4	0.3	1.7	(0.9)	(1.1)	0.5	0.7	1.8
Error	0.4	0.3	0.8	0.5	0.2	0.4	0.3	0.2

Note: These data are related in the following way:

Private sector savings/investment balance + government balance = current-account balance

Source: Calculated from data in Economic Planning Agency, *Annual Report on National Accounts*.

they allowed investment and economic growth to occur without foreign borrowing. However, problems arose when the growth rate dropped in the 1970s. Put simply, the society continued to generate high levels of savings, but these were no longer matched by a strong private-sector demand for investment; lower growth requires less new investment each year than high growth. Therefore, the private sector of the economy began to generate a considerable excess of savings over investment. Over the past decade, that surplus has ranged from 3 percent to over 6 percent of GNP, a sizable imbalance. Table 2 summarizes the changes.

Neither the lower levels of private-sector investment nor the high levels of private-sector savings appear likely to change in the near future. Corporate investment demand will continue to be constrained by the end of the technology gap with the West, while personal investment will not pick up unless there is substantial change in government policy to encourage housing. Corporate savings will be governed by profits and depreciation rules, with few dramatic increases likely, and personal savings may continue at a high level. There is currently a debate in Japan over the impact of an aging population on personal savings, with some expectation that the rapidly increasing proportion of elderly in the population (who are assumed to dissave) will bring down the average saving ratio. However, this trend could be easily counterbalanced by increased anxiety over the future level of support that people anticipate from government social security and by concerns that postretirement employment opportunities will become more scarce.

The surplus of private-sector savings over investment must be absorbed elsewhere in the system, either through a government-sector deficit (spending more than it receives in tax revenues and funding the rest through bond issues that soak up private-sector savings) or through a net flow of savings abroad. Both have occurred in Japan over the past decade. If neither government deficits nor capital outflow had accommodated the savings imbalance, other economic forces would have pushed savings and investment back toward each other.

Most of the surplus savings in the private sector have actually been absorbed by government deficit spending, as shown in Table 2. These deficits expanded to 5.5 percent of GNP by 1978 because of both deliberate policy decisions to increase spending on many social programs and an unanticipated drop in the growth of government tax revenue due to slower economic growth. Alarmed at the size of these deficits and bolstered by private-sector demands for greater efficiency in government to be demonstrated by smaller deficits (the administrative reform movement), the Ministry of Finance embarked on a campaign to bring down the size of the government deficit through a combination of tax increases and strict controls on spending. The macroeconomic implication was that the government of Japan was no longer willing to absorb as much of

11

the surplus private-sector savings as in the past. Since 1978, the size of the government deficit relative to GNP has dropped by almost half, to 3.5 percent in 1983 (and probably close to 3 percent in 1984 and 1985).

Since government deficits have not absorbed all of the surplus savings in Japan, a net outflow of savings to the rest of the world has accounted for the rest. But here, too, the principle that everything must be accounted for applies: what leaves the country must equal what enters the country, so that the outflow of savings also means a current-account surplus. Over the past decade, Japan has not had a large current-account surplus on average because the period has been punctuated by the two oil shocks (which caused a temporary reversal of the trends) and because of the rapid expansion of government deficits. However, the current-account surplus and capital outflow have risen as a share of GNP as the excess private-sector savings have continued and the government has absorbed less of them. The outflow shifted from a deficit of 1.1 percent in 1980 to a surplus of 1.8 percent in 1983 (see Table 2).

A fundamental and important conclusion may be drawn from this discussion: macroeconomic factors in Japan have brought about chronic, large current-account surpluses. In 1984, Japan's surplus was $35 billion, or approximately 3 percent of GNP, a level which expanded to $49 billion or just under 4 percent in 1985. All indications are that large surpluses will continue for a number of years, even though the results in 1984 and 1985 may be unusually high.

The current account in the balance of payments is composed of merchandise trade, services and unilateral transfers (primarily foreign aid). Since Japan is a foreign aid donor it has a deficit on transfers. It has also traditionally had a deficit on services, so that the merchandise trade surpluses have been even larger than the total current-account surpluses. Within merchandise trade, Japan has chronic deficits with those countries, such as the OPEC nations, that supply it with large amounts of raw materials, offset by very large surpluses with most other trading partners. All the countries included in this study have trade deficits with Japan, a fact that has considerable importance in shaping the economic issues between Japan and the region.

From 1979 until 1985, the political support for driving down the size of government deficits, a policy which has brought about the strong increase in Japan's current-account surpluses, was very broad and committed. It was difficult to find a government official, any politician belonging to the ruling Liberal Democratic Party, or a leading businessman who would argue for fiscal stimulus during this period. But by the fall of 1985 the first cracks were beginning to appear in that support. The slowdown in the U.S. economy, coupled with the rise in the value of the yen against the dollar resulting from concerted international intervention in exchange markets by central banks beginning in September,

12

meant that Japan's exports were growing more slowly and thereby doing less to pull along the rest of the economy. Policymakers were thus more willing to consider ways to stimulate domestic demand. Much of the new discussion revolved around deregulating industry and other actions that would not involve government spending, but the prospect for such policies bringing any measurable contribution to economic growth was dim. Some people were willing to admit that fiscal stimulus (that is, increasing the size of the government deficit) would be necessary to prevent a serious drop in economic growth. Supporters of such a policy fell into the familiar routine of encouraging the U.S. government to pressure Japan to adopt such policies. In January 1986 the Japanese press reported that the country would surely be criticized at the industrial nation summit to be held in Tokyo that May for its failure to stimulate the domestic economy. Some criticism did materialize and by mid-year Japan was edging toward fiscal stimulus, especially after the release of statistics indicating a drop in GNP in the first quarter.

Foreign Economic Policy

The process of economic growth and development in Japan was characterized by what economists term import substitution, and what a political scientist might term nationalism. Japanese industry, with strong government encouragement, eagerly developed domestic substitutes for imported products. In the 1950s, the government erected stiff barriers against imports, including both high tariffs and stringent quotas. In addition, the Ministry of International Trade and Industry was given authority over the allocation of foreign exchange, so that any corporation needing foreign currency to purchase imports had to obtain the ministry's approval first. These controls meant that Japan was virtually a closed market for many foreign manufactured goods. Consumer products were largely kept out as unnecessary luxuries, and any product competing with a fledgling Japanese industry was blocked on the basis of infant industry protection.

Import barriers were reinforced by investment restrictions. Foreign companies that tried to circumvent the import barriers by establishing manufacturing subsidiaries in Japan found that route virtually closed as well. Foreign companies were allowed to invest only through joint ventures (in which their ownership was 50 percent or less) or by agreeing not to repatriate their profits.

This policy of severely restricting imports and investment is often described as a highly intelligent industrial policy that benefits those industries singled out for growth. In reality, virtually every industry in Japan that faced competition from abroad was protected. Japanese industries thus were able to develop behind this strong protectionist wall until they could compete internationally. This takes us back to the ele-

13

mentary principle that competition is good for the economy: Import barriers decrease competition, and far too often countries find that protection only produces perenially inefficient firms that have lost the incentive to increase productivity. Japan, however, tended to be successful in generating efficient firms because there was still sufficient competition among domestic firms in major industries to drive rapid innovation and productivity growth. By maintaining trade barriers, Japan interfered with another basic economic principle: comparative advantage. It would have been better off to allow free trade but it chose to accept the temporary inefficiency of trade barriers in hopes of a longer-term gain from building strong domestic firms.

Although the policy of heavy import protection certainly benefited many Japanese companies, it had another rationale as well. When the exchange rate was fixed in 1949 at ¥360 = $1, it was overvalued, meaning that Japan had trouble exporting enough to pay for its imports. Under the Bretton Woods system, countries were supposed to adopt policies to defend their exchange rates at the established parities and resort to devaluation only as a final step. Japan was even more committed to maintaining its exchange rate than most nations because of a strong desire to prove to the world that it was a worthy member of the international economic system after its disastrous international behavior of the 1930s and 1940s. Therefore, it was eager to fulfill its obligations under the system by adopting policies that would help keep the current account from falling too far into deficit. The United States found Japan's behavior acceptable for the same reason. Severe restrictions on imports were a major part of the policy package used to achieve this result.

By the 1960s, the need to defend Japanese industries and the exchange rate through stiff import barriers was rapidly disappearing, and the willingness of countries like the United States to tolerate the restrictions was evaporating. In 1963, Japan began a piecemeal process of dismantling import barriers that has continued to the present. As a result of the changes, official barriers to imports are now rather low in Japan. Relatively few items are still subject to quota restrictions (and almost all of them are agricultural products), and the *average* tariff level is the lowest among industrial nations. Nevertheless, some products of great interest to American exporters are still under quotas or high tariffs. In addition, imports continue to be adversely affected by a variety of other problems, such as product standards that are deliberately designed to keep foreign goods out (or inadvertently have that effect) and informal pressure from the government to limit purchases from abroad. These barriers are extemely difficult to quantify, but American companies do experience real problems in exporting to Japan. Some progress has been

14

made in negotiating away these nontariff barriers, but room remains for improvement.

This consistent movement toward greater openness for imports has been beneficial for Japan and its trading partners, allowing the principle of comparative advantage described in the introduction to operate more fully. Nevertheless, the process of opening has been an agonizing one, with Japan responding only to strong threats and pressure from abroad. Japan has not had a strong domestic constituency for trade liberalization that could lobby for these changes independently from foreign pressure. Even those groups that have supported greater openness have generally based their arguments on the need to demonstrate sufficient commitment to liberal trade to prevent other nations from instituting protection against Japan's exports.

Despite the more emotionally charged international trade climate and the stronger criticisms of Japan, domestic attitudes do not appear to be changing. In the fall of 1985, most Japanese I met continued to support trade liberalization to avoid retaliation by foreign nations against Japan's exports. Such retaliation, it was thought, would hurt export industries and cause Japan's economic growth to suffer. With only one exception, the people with whom I discussed these issues failed to mention that liberalization was good because it would make the Japanese economy more efficient and benefit consumers. As long as the argument is presented mainly in terms of maintaining access to export markets, Japan's domestic lobby for liberalization must have foreign threats as its primary mechanism for achieving change. This is an extremely unfortunate state of affairs, and one that has important implications for Japan's relations around the region.

Summary

Japan has grown rapidly to become a major advanced industrial nation which, by virtue of its economic size, has an important role to play in Northeast Asia. However, the Japanese growth engine has slowed considerably from the wild days of the 1950s and 1960s, with no prospect of a return to those levels. Lower growth, combined with continued high savings and a government reluctant to absorb those savings through sizable government deficits, has also meant large trade surpluses with the rest of the world. These surpluses are a sore point with Japan's major trading partners. Attitudes toward economic Japan and its surpluses have also been adversely affected by the lack of enthusiasm Japan has shown toward playing a leadership role in the world trade system, as evidenced by its reluctance to accept trade liberalization at home. These facts raise a number of questions that need to be addressed in looking at Japan's relations with other Northeast Asian countries.

15

First, is there a way to step back from the daily deluge of problems and complaints in order to evaluate the overall contribution of Japan to the economies of the region? There is no convenient, simple way to measure this, but the following pages will explain the multidimensional nature of Japan's interaction.

Second, to what extent is Japan a model for other countries in the region? Despite the many cultural and historical differences between Japan and the developing nations of the region, the fact remains that Japan is the one Asian country that has successfully industrialized.

Third, is there concern elsewhere in the region about the austere fiscal policies that have contributed to Japan's large current-account surpluses? Would the atmosphere surrounding the discussion of specific trade issues be improved if macroeconomic policy in Japan led to smaller surpluses?

Fourth, will Japan move rapidly enough in addressing its own barriers to imports to convince its trading partners that the current system of world trade rules should remain intact? This depends on both Japan's ability to respond to pressures and the degree of frustration among its trading partners.

III. The U.S.-Japan Relationship

Because the two countries engage in so much bilateral trade, the economic relationship between Japan and the United States dominates all others in Northeast Asia and sets many of the parameters for those other relations. It is useful to separate the economic developments in the U.S.-Japan relations from the policy problems.

Economic Background

The macroeconomic developments in Japan have already been described. In the United States, macroeconomic policy has moved the nation in exactly the opposite direction as Japan. Unlike Japan, the United States does not generate high'levels of private-sector savings. Therefore, the very large government deficits brought about by Reagan administration fiscal policy, combined with the private-sector demand for investment funds, have exceeded the supply of savings available in the economy. The United States has thus had to borrow from abroad, which has generated current-account deficits. From a small surplus on current account of $4.6 billion in 1981, the balance deteriorated to a deficit of $102 billion in 1984. With the United States pursuing policies that pushed it into large global deficits and Japan pursuing policies that led to record surpluses, it is no surprise that bilateral trade shows a heavy surplus for Japan.

Other economic factors have also contributed to bilateral imbalance. Even when the United States has had global surpluses and Japan global deficits, the bilateral balance has been in Japan's favor. The economic reason for this is Japan's position as a major raw material importer. Since Japan has large deficits with raw material suppliers, it must run surpluses with other nations even to have a zero global trade balance. Therefore, Japan has tended to have surpluses with the United States and the other nations of Northeast Asia because none of them is a major raw material supplier.

From a deficit with Japan in 1980 of $9.9 billion (a year when Japan had a global deficit), the U.S. bilateral trade imbalance grew to $46 billion in 1985 (see Table 3). With the $10 billion level of 1980 as a crude figure for the base-level imbalance due to Japan's position as a raw material importer, the deterioration of the bilateral imbalance follows from the strong and opposite moves in the global balances of the two countries, especially since 1982.

If both Japan and the United States continue their macroeconomic policies of the early 1980s, the inescapable outcome will be for contin-

Table 3
Trade Balances, Japan and the United States
($ billions)

Year	U.S. Global Trade Balance[a]	Japanese Global Trade Balance[b]	Bilateral Trade[c]
1980	$(24.5)	$(10.7)	$ (9.9)
1981	(27.2)	8.7	(15.8)
1982	(31.7)	6.9	(16.8)
1983	(57.5)	20.5	(19.3)
1984	—	33.6	(33.6)
1985	—	46.1	(46.2)

[a] Exports measured f.a.s (fast alongside ship), imports measured on customs value basis.
[b] Exports measured f.o.b.; imports c.i.f.
[c] U.S. data, measured as in note a.
Sources: Department of Commerce, *Survey of Current Business*; Bank of Japan, *Balance of Payments Monthly*.

ued large bilateral trade imbalances. Cracks were appearing in the firm commitment to fiscal austerity in Japan late in 1985, and Japan could begin to move in a more expansionary direction during 1986. In the United States as well, the Gramm-Rudman-Hollings bill mandating measures to balance the federal budget that was passed into law at the end of 1985 indicated a change in policy. Nevertheless, such changes are taking place at a slow pace, ensuring a continuing pattern of Japanese surplus and U.S. deficit for the near future.

A side issue in the understanding of macroeconomic developments is the role of exchange rates. Much was made of the decision by the finance ministers of the Group of Five on September 22, 1985, to push down the value of the dollar against the yen and European currencies. Many saw that policy decision as leading to a smaller Japanese surplus and U.S. deficit. The actual movement in exchange rates has been surprisingly large and sustained, with the yen appreciating approximately 20 percent against the dollar from September to December 1985 and an additional 27 percent by June 1986. However, it is wrong to assume that intervention in exchange markets alone can solve the imbalances. Exchange rates are prices that bring about equality of international demand and supply for currencies, and they are driven by macroeconomic forces. In the case of Japan, the "weak" yen that prevailed over the past several years was the necessary price to generate the current-account surplus and capital outflow to balance the domestic surplus savings. The currency was weak in the sense that American industries felt that they faced excessive competition from Japanese products, but it was a correct level to bring about the required macroeconomic balance. The same argument could

18

be made for the United States: the strong dollar was the exchange price required to bring about current-account deficits and capital inflow to balance the domestic excess demand for funds.

The above statements imply that an independent move to alter the exchange rate ought to be doomed to failure. Since this has not been the case, macroeconomic conditions must have changed in ways to support the intervention in the markets. Specifically, the Bank of Japan pushed interest rates up in the fall of 1985 to make domestic investment more attractive relative to foreign investments. If more investors choose to keep their savings in Japan, the demand for foreign currencies decreases and the yen will rise in value. However, in a longer perspective, the higher value of the yen means that Japan's trade surplus will shrink. Unless the government is prepared to increase fiscal stimulus to provide the necessary expansion of domestic demand to absorb that surplus at home, other economic forces could push the yen back down again. Once again, it is important to remember that everything must be accounted for: Japan has a current-account surplus because the society produces more than it wants to buy at home and the exchange rate is weak; if that surplus is to shrink, the domestic economy must absorb relatively more. The only practical way to absorb more at home is through increased deficit spending by the government.

This macroeconomic side of the bilateral relationship is important because the size of the bilateral trade imbalance is often used as a rationale either to press Japan to reduce its trade barriers or to limit its access to American markets. Few people recognize, however, that the size of the imbalance results from macroeconomic conditions and policy responses of both governments, not from trade barriers in either country. Whether this distinction is recognized or not, the tone of bilateral dialogue has been tense over the past few years. On the one hand, American corporations have been facing stronger competition from Japan over the past two decades as Japan has grown and developed. Starting with textiles in the 1950s, Japan has moved up the industrial ladder to become a major competitive world exporter in steel and ship-building in the 1960s and then consumer electronics and automobiles in the 1970s and 1980s. American companies have reacted to this rising competition with a combination of fear, envy and bitterness and have used American trade laws to inhibit imports from Japan when possible.

On the other hand, every American administration since the mid-1960s has been engaged in the struggle to get Japan to lower its own import barriers. As described earlier, this has been a long, slow, unpleasant process. Over time, American frustrations have become worse, culminating in a unanimous Senate resolution in March 1985 condemning Japan's behavior on imports and calling on the president to use protectionism as a retaliatory tool to force Japan to change. Resolutions do not carry the weight of law, which may explain the unanimous vote, but the March action remains a vivid expression of the discontent, anger and frustration with Japan that prevails in Washington. During 1985, some fifty bills were introduced to Congress that would have adversely affected Japan, some of them advocating the imposition of tariffs on all imports from Japan. None of these bills passed, but the trend is disturbing.

Why are relations so fraught with problems and ill will? The following reasons capture the main features of the problem:

1. Japan is a large, successful industrial country that constitutes the major foreign competition for many American companies. It is inevitable that there will be problems in this case, if for no other reason than that U.S. trade law provides a variety of circumstances in which protectionist relief from foreign competition can be legally justified. In this sense, the problems with Japan are a sign of the closeness of the two countries' economic ties.

2. Japan's foreign economic policies have been very defensive. As discussed above, Japan lacks a domestic constituency for liberal trade, and it rarely takes the initiative in raising issues with the United States. Therefore, the bulk of the news in the bilateral relationship is generated in Washington. Since the United States is by far the largest trading partner for Japan, U.S. government officials have borne the brunt of the work in pressuring Japan to lower its import barriers. This effort necessarily generates negative news.

3. The defensiveness just described contributes further to American frustration because of our belief that Japan should now be a *leader* of the international liberal trading system. According to this view, because Japan has become a strong surplus country, it should assume the leadership role in the international economic community that the United States played in the 1950s and 1960s. Because Japan does not play a more constructive role, American frustration rises further.

4. Culturally, U.S. negotiators find the Japanese very difficult to deal with. The Japanese penchant for arguing endlessly over what Americans see as minute, obscure, unimportant details is annoying. Even people with previous experience or training on Japan are quickly frustrated when they enter government and must spend weary, fruitless hours at the negotiating table. Those frustrations are both vented to the press and incorporated in harsher U.S. policy responses.

Despite the frustrations, bilateral negotiations have resulted in a large number of unilateral Japanese concessions. The Reagan administration entered office with a clearly stated goal of pushing Japan on its import barriers rather than reacting through increased protection in the United States. The imposition of restrictions on automobile imports and other decisions have tarnished that goal, but the administration has certainly

20

worked hard in negotiating with Japan. The results from any particular set of negotiations may appear minor, but added up over the five years, the accomplishments are fairly substantial. Tariffs have been lowered, quota restrictions have been eased, and problems with standards and inspection requirements have been improved.

Summary

Several features of the U.S.-Japan relationship and its implications for Japan's relations with Northeast Asia stand out. First, the depth of the frustration with Japan evident in Washington is striking and becoming more serious. Although there is a big difference between Senate resolutions and binding laws, the willingness to speak out harshly against Japan is certainly increasing. Even those people and groups traditionally favoring free trade find it difficult to say kind words about Japan. Consider, for example, the fact that Senator John Danforth, who introduced the resolution in the Senate to restrict trade, is considered to be a moderate on trade issues.

Second, the United States does appear to have carried most of the burden of negotiating with Japan. In many instances other countries ride on the coat tails of the United States, taking up similar issues with Japan once the United States has made the initial push. However, as will be considered later, smaller Asian countries face some difficulties with this.

Third, there has been a surprising lack of interest or discussion concerning macroeconomic issues. Trade officials and politicians focus on the size of the bilateral trade imbalance, but few recognize the need to address macroeconomic policy as part of the solution. Perhaps the unwillingness has been governed by the Reagan administration's inability to curtail deficits in the United States until 1986, so that it was not in a strong position to tell Japan what to do. In addition, Reagan administration economic officials may have felt uncomfortable with the policy prescription for Japan — fiscal stimulus through larger government deficits. That policy was incompatible with the monetarist economists' own beliefs. For whatever reason, both countries pursued domestic fiscal policies without regard for their international implications. That this appeared to be changing by late 1985 was at least an encouraging sign.

21

IV. Northeast Asia

Northeast Asia consists of a number of countries tied together principally by geography and by some common cultural elements. Comparison of national income levels is difficult because of the shifts in exchange rates over time, but it still has some usefulness (see Table 4). The United States and Japan stand far ahead of all the other nations in the region; behind them come a group of middle income developing countries, ranging from the Soviet Union and Hong Kong at a per capita income of $5,000 – 7,000 to Taiwan and South Korea at $2,000 – 3,000. China sits at the bottom as the least developed, with an estimated per capita GNP of only $300.

Not only is there great disparity in income levels, but even the economic and political systems vary from one end of the spectrum to the other. The United States and Japan are large democratic nations with capitalist economic systems in which the government plays a relatively restrained economic role. All governments are involved with the economy in a variety of ways, but in these two countries, indicators such as the size of the government sector relative to the rest of the economy show government to be less intrusive than it is in most others. Hong Kong, a small colony of a democratic nation (to revert to Chinese ownership in 1997), also prides itself on the relatively small role of government. Taiwan and South Korea are quasi-democratic capitalist countries with a generally stronger government role in economic affiars. The Soviet Union, Mongolia and North Korea are socialist countries with rigid systems of central planning. China, on the other hand, is a socialist country engaged in bold experiments that combine elements of central planning and features of markets and local economic decision-making.

The disparity in income level and economic and political systems is so great that geography seems to be the only binding element in Northeast Asia. Economically, though, most of the developing countries in the region have a common thread in the form of rapid economic growth. A review of Table 1 reveals that the principal developing countries of the region have produced GNP growth rates ranging from 6 to 9 percent in the last decade despite the less favorable international economic environment. In addition, some general comments apply to all or most countries of the region, including the strength of the Japan relationship, the bilateral trade imbalances, Japan's role as a capital supplier, foreign aid, technology, and the dominance of the U.S. bilateral relationship.

Table 4
Comparison of National Income Levels
per capita GNP
(in U.S. Dollars)

	1983
United States	$14,110
Japan	10,120
Hong Kong	5,370
Taiwan	2,742
South Korea	2,010
North Korea	923
China	335
USSR	6,981
Mongolia	—

Note: Taiwan data for 1984 and converted at average rate reported by Taiwanese data.
Sources: World Bank, *World Development Report*, 1985, pp. 174–75; *Taiwan Statistical Data Book; Asia Yearbook, 1985* (for China and North Korea); and Central Intelligence Agency, *Handbook of Economic Statistics*, 1985.

The Strength of Economic Ties

Table 5 presents data on U.S. and Japanese trade with the countries of Northeast Asia. Japan is the largest single source of imports for three of the six countries, and Hong Kong should be added to that list on the grounds that many of its imports from China are simply passed through Hong Kong for reexport. Even for the United States, Canada exceeds Japan as a source of imports by only a small margin. Only the Soviet Union does not fit the pattern, with the United States and several European countries outranking Japan as its trading partners. With the above exception, Japan is thus the major supplier of goods to the other countries of the region, and since Japan has no raw materials to export, these are all manufactured products.

On the export side, the relationship is not as strong. Although Japan is a sizeable export market for these countries, absorbing 10 to 20 percent of the exports of all except Hong Kong and the Soviet Union, it is the largest single export market for none. Again, that picture alters slightly if the China/Hong Kong relationship is ignored; since China exports coal and oil, Japan is its major overseas market.

These data also point strikingly to one of Japan's major image problems: it stands out as the largest supplier to most of these countries but falls far behind the United States as a buyer. Bilateral imbalances between Japan and Northeast Asian countries other than the United States

23

Table 5

U.S. and Japanese Trade in the Region, 1984

($ millions)

	Total	Exports to U.S.	to Japan	Total	Imports from U.S	from Japan	Trade Balance with Japan
United States	$217,890	—	$23,575	$341,179	—	$60,371	$36,796
Japan	169,700	$60,429[b]	—	136,072	$26,887[b]	—	—
South Korea	28,090	10,195[b]	4,464	30,796	6,962	7,656[b]	3,192
Taiwan	30,456	8,759[b]	3,186	21,959	5,042	6,441[b]	3,255
China	24,824	2,313	5,155[c]	21,313	2,753	5,495[b]	340
Hong Kong	28,318	9,405[b]	1,251	24,011	2,637	5,516[c]	4,265
Soviet Union[a]	32,816	546	1,262	34,897	3,284	2,515	1,253

[a] The numbers for the Soviet Union are calculated by the IMF, based on data supplied by member countries and thereby excluding trade with most members of the Soviet bloc.

[b] Largest single destination (origin) for exports (imports).

[c] The relationship would be the largest if China's exports to Hong Kong (many of which are simply reexported) are excluded.

Source: International Monetary Fund, Direction of Trade Statistics, Yearbook 1985; Council for Economic Planning, Republic of China, Taiwan Statistical Data Book, 1985.

range from $340 million for China to $4.3 billion for Hong Kong. China's small imbalance deteriorated rapidly in 1985, reaching $2.3 billion in the first half of the year.

Before jumping to conclusions about Japan's unwillingness to play an adequate role in buying the exports of these countries, recall the macro-economic and other structural features of Japan's trade. That Japan has a surplus with these countries is a logical outcome of its extensive raw material dependence and its rising global trade surpluses. Even though economists can find a logical rationale, data such as these do feed the negative impression that Japan is a reluctant buyer.

Another significant feature in Table 5 is that the United States has by no means been eliminated by the competition from Japan. Despite the advantages of Japan's geographical proximity and supposed cultural affinity to Northeast Asia and the high dollar/weak yen, the United States did not lag very far behind Japan in most of these markets. Considering that these data are for 1984, the culmination of several years of a very strong dollar, this is a generally strong showing. Extremists occasionally speak of Japan's economic role as a re-creation of the exclusive "co-prosperity sphere" of the war years. These data belie such a notion. This point will be evident again later in reviewing the situation regarding particular countries.

Capital Flows

Offsetting Japan's surpluses with the countries of Northeast Asia is a net flow of capital. It is also useful, however, to look at the gross flows taking place. Many people tend to think of capital flows in terms of foreign direct investment — the direct investment by corporations in their subsidiaries (both joint ventures and wholly owned operations) abroad. Although a highly visible form of investment, this is only one form of capital flow. In the case of Japan, foreign direct investment constitutes only about 10 percent of total gross investment abroad. The rest takes place in the form of portfolio investment in the equities of foreign companies, investment in bonds (and other debt instruments) issued by foreign companies and governments, plus the loans made abroad by Japanese financial institutions or the trade credit extended abroad by Japanese corporations. Unfortunately, regional or country-specific data on these activities do not exist except in the case of direct investment. Those data that do exist indicate that a rather small share of Japan's overseas investments is in Northeast Asia.

In terms of foreign direct investment, Japan's involvement with the region is strong and clear, but it has been decreasing in a relative sense over time. When Japanese companies first began investing in overseas operations, they tended to move to countries in Asia to take advantage of low wages. But as their horizons expanded, and as the Japanese

25

government's regulations restricting outward investment gradually disappeared, the direction of foreign direct investment has shifted. By the end of 1983, 7.5 percent of Japan's total investment was in Northeast Asia, compared to 26.8 percent invested in the United States (see Table 6).

The United States is becoming more important in Japan's foreign direct investment. In fiscal-year 1983, almost one-third of new direct investment went to the United States, while the Northeast Asian countries rose slightly to 10 percent. Rather than detaching itself from its close relationship with the United States, Japan appears to be moving even closer.

Another revealing feature about Japan's role in the region comes from comparing U.S. and Japanese investment. Although disparities in the method of calculating these data prevent a direct comparison of the amounts of investment by each in Asian countries, they do show that a much larger share of Japan's investment goes to Asia than is the case for the United States. As of the end of 1983, less than 6 percent of U.S. foreign direct investment was in Asian countries (both Southeast and Northeast Asia) compared to 27 percent of Japan's investment. In that sense, the region is relatively more important to Japan than to the United States.

South Korea and Taiwan provide their own data on inward direct investment, which allow comparison between U.S. and Japanese investment there. For South Korea, 47 percent of direct investment through 1984 has been by the Japanese and 31 percent by the United States. In Taiwan for the same period, approximately 22 percent of inward investment is from Japan while 31 percent is from the United

Table 6
Japan's Foreign Direct Investment
(cumulative investment through 1983, in $ millions)

	Amount	Share
Total	$58,611	
United States	15,707	26.8%
Northeast Asia	4,396	7.5
Soviet Union	193	0.3
South Korea	1,436	2.5
Taiwan	531	0.9
Hong Kong	2,165	3.7
China	71	0.1

Source: Ministry of Finance, *Okurasho Kokusai Kin'yukyoku Nenkan*, 1984.

States. Taiwan may not be representative of other countries in the region, but these figures do demonstrate the relative strength of the United States once again. While Japan is an important, sizable investor, so is the United States.

Because of the lack of data, generalizations about other forms of capital flow are also difficult to make. However, at a broad level, the World Bank has pointed out Japan's rising role in lending to developing countries. According to its *World Development Report 1985*, developing countries accounted for 24 percent of the total yen-denominated foreign bonds issued in Japan as of the end of 1983, with bonds issued by the international development banks accounting for an additional 24 percent. Unofficial data obtained during the research mission further indicate that just under 3 percent of the outstanding balance of yen-denominated foreign bonds as of the end of March 1985 had been issued by South Korea and China, which would account for about 12 percent of the share issued by all developing countries in Japan.

Besides the flotation of bonds in Japan, the World Bank data show that 49 percent of all medium- and long-term loan commitments abroad made by Japanese banks in 1983 were to oil-importing developing countries, and the figure has been above 30 percent every year since 1980. According to unofficial data obtained during the research mission, approximately 4 percent of the outstanding balance on commercial bank loans extended overseas went to South Korea, while China obtained 0.3 percent and Taiwan 0.1 percent. Since much of Japanese bank lending is to Japanese subsidiaries operating in foreign countries, or to local companies purchasing equipment from Japan, a lowering of investment and trade barriers in the other countries would bring about an expanded amount of financing from Japan as well.

These developments have been aided by the gradual deregulation of Japan's financial markets over the past decade. Until the late 1960s, the Ministry of Finance maintained a strong web of controls over all forms of foreign exchange transactions, which impeded the international flow of capital into and out of Japan. Since that time, though, the Japanese government has engaged in a slow but relatively continuous process of deregulating international transactions, to the point where Japan has now become a major international financial center. Access to Japan's capital markets is most important to debtor countries like South Korea and China.

Many of the figures cited above suggest that from Japan's perspective the capital flow to Northeast Asian developing countries is small relative to the total capital outflow. This result is affected by both the dominance of the United States as a destination for Japanese capital and the role of lending intermediaries like the World Bank.

27

Foreign Aid

Japan is the world's major donor of bilateral foreign aid to Asian countries (that is, aid distributed directly by Japan to individual countries rather than to multilateral aid agencies like the World Bank), and the region receives a major portion of total Japanese aid expenditures. Since 1980, the proportion of bilateral aid going to Asia as a whole has slowly declined from 70 percent to 66 percent as Japan's horizon has expanded to other parts of the world (see Table 7). In fact, the total amount of bilateral aid has not expanded rapidly, and the amount spent in Asia has actually declined marginally when measured in dollars. This has happened for two reasons: the dollar appreciated modestly against the yen between 1980 and 1984 (from ¥226 = $1 to ¥237 = $1), and Japan emphasized increased donations to multilateral organizations rather than increased bilateral activity after 1982. While the bilateral aid going to Asia increased only 15 percent in dollar terms over this period, the amount of multilateral aid increased 41 percent. Much of this money may also end up in Asia, but through a more indirect route.

Once the focus is narrowed to Northeast Asia, foreign aid is generally a less important component of Japan's economic relationship. Hong Kong does not receive aid, and Taiwan has not received any since 1972, part of the price of Japan's recognition of China. The Soviet Union, North Korea and Mongolia are outside the realm of foreign aid. This leaves South Korea and China as the aid recipients within the region. China has topped the list of recipients of Japanese aid every year since 1982. South Korea dropped off the list of the top ten recipients after 1981, but an agreement reached in 1983 to supply Korea with $4 billion in aid over a number of years may move it back onto the list.

Table 7
Japan's Official Development Assistance
($ millions)

Year	Total	Multilateral	Bilateral Total	Asia Amount	Asia Share
1980	$3,304	$1,343	$1,961	$1,383	70.5%
1981	3,171	911	2,260	1,605	71.0
1982	3,023	656	2,367	1,624	68.6
1983	3,761	1,336	2,425	1,614	66.5
1984	4,319	1,892	2,427	1,594	65.7

Source: Japan Economic Institute, *JEI Report,* no. 33A, September 2, 1983, and no. 44A, November 15, 1985.

Japan's foreign aid spending in the future will continue to grow relatively rapidly, but it faces some constraints due to the atmosphere of fiscal austerity. Foreign aid has been exempted from the overall spending limitations introduced by the Ministry of Finance in 1979, but it still has not grown as rapidly as once envisioned. At the beginning of the 1980s, the Japanese government set a goal of doubling foreign aid over the 1981–1985 period, which proved to be untenable. In the fall of 1985, that forecast was replaced with a somewhat more conservative one of doubling aid over the seven-year period to 1992.

Regardless of the ability to meet any particular targets for increasing aid, what matters most is that Japan is one of the largest aid donors in the world (ranking fourth in 1983 at $3.0 billion), continues to increase its aid spending relatively rapidly and spends most of that money in Asia. The quality of Japanese aid has also improved over time, with the proportion of untied aid in bilateral aid rising rapidly.

Narrowing the focus somewhat further, it is important to realize that official development assistance (ODA) consists of both grants and loans. In Japan, the loan component of ODA comes from the Overseas Economic Cooperation Fund (OECF), which lends money at concessionary interest rates. Its program includes loans both to governments and to Japanese companies involved in qualified projects in developing countries, although this second activity comprises less than 10 percent of all OECF lending. China accounted for 12 percent of the lending to governments in 1983, while South Korea accounted for 8 percent. None of the Northeast Asian countries receives a significant share of the program of loans to Japanese corporations.

How can all of these facts and figures be summarized? Japan has emerged as a major foreign aid donor in the world, but aid is not relevant for all of the countries in Northeast Asia. For South Korea and China, though, Japan is an important source of assistance, both directly and through multilateral organizations. If Japan has problems in its role as an aid donor, they appear to be in the form of its low profile and commercial orientation. Few Japanese are employed in the World Bank and other multilateral organizations, and most of them are on loan from Japanese ministries or government-affiliated organizations. At the OECF, the tendency is to respond to foreign requests in a passive manner rather than initiating or coordinating a strong, active aid policy for any particular country. Mechanisms for coordinating foreign aid among the OECF and other agencies are relatively weak. Japan used to be criticized for the high portion of tied aid or aid granted on condition that it be used to purchase particular products exported from Japan. Although the untied portion of its aid has increased, Japan is still subjected to some criticism for the relatively low portion of grants compared to loans in its ODA.

Technology

As Japan has become a major technological leader in the world, it has played a greater role in the transfer of technology to other countries. This change is not entirely evident from balance-of-payments data because Japan's experience of importing technology itself is so recent that it continues to have a very large net deficit of payments for licensing agreements. But the point remains valid that Japan is becoming a significant source of technology around the world.

Table 8 demonstrates what has happened. For the decade from 1973 to 1982, total receipts for licensing technology abroad more than tripled, for an annual growth of 15 percent. The share of licensing receipts from Asian countries in total receipts remains closer to 40 percent, even as sophisticated Japanese technology has become of relatively greater interest to American and European firms.

Among Northeast Asian countries, however, the picture is different. Receipts from Taiwan and South Korea have shown little increase since 1979, and those from China have declined substantially since a peak in 1978. Although these data may indicate some reluctance to transfer technology to potential competitors, they may also simply reflect the inadequacy of data measurement. Formal licensing agreements are only one form of transfer; Japan is also playing a role through educational programs, through knowledge transferred within Japanese direct investments and public-domain knowledge generated in Japan.

Table 8
Japan's Technology Licensing Receipts
(¥ billions)

Fiscal Year	Total	Asia			
		Total	China	Taiwan	South Korea
1973	¥ 50.8	¥20.8	¥ 4.7	¥ —	¥3.4
1974	57.1	19.2	4.2	2.7	5.2
1975	66.5	26.1	2.7	2.9	4.7
1976	83.4	32.0	7.5	4.7	7.0
1977	93.3	29.8	1.7	5.1	6.3
1978	122.0	38.4	10.2	4.2	7.6
1979	133.1	54.8	19.2	8.6	7.8
1980	159.6	54.2	9.5	9.9	5.3
1981	175.1	67.9	4.8	12.0	9.5
1982	184.9	70.8	4.5	9.7	7.5

Source: Science and Technology Agency, *Kagaku Gijutsu Hakusho* (Science and Technology White Paper), 1978 and 1984.

Dominance of the U.S.-Japan Relationship

From the perspective of Japan, the relationship with the United States is of overwhelming importance. This is an unbalanced dependency, for Japan has a far less distinctive role in the international economic ties of the United States. The United States was the destination for 35 percent of Japan's exports in 1984, while the United States sent only 11 percent of its exports to Japan. On the import side the relationship is more balanced, with 18 percent of U.S. imports coming from Japan, and the reverse flow representing 20 percent of Japan's imports (see Table 9).

Direct investment provides a more dramatic contrast. Only 4 percent of foreign direct investment (FDI) by U.S. firms is located in Japan, whereas 27 percent of FDI by Japanese firms is in the United States. Conversely, 9 percent of the inward direct investment in the United States is by Japanese firms, whereas fully 54 percent of inward investment in Japan is by U.S. firms.

Over time some of these relative dependencies have strengthened and others weakened, but the general imbalance has remained. If anything, the rising share of both Japan's exports and its foreign investment to the United States indicates that Japan's relative dependence on the United States has increased.

The Japanese are well aware of their strong dependence on the U.S. economy. In the 1960s economists talked about Japan getting sick every time the United States sneezed, and the ties have not weakened since. It is thus not surprising that the United States is covered so heavily by the Japanese news media.

Table 9
U.S.-Japan Economic Interdependence

	1973	1984
Trade		
Japan's share in U.S. exports	12%	11%
Japan's share in U.S. imports	14	18
U.S. share in Japan's exports	26	35
U.S. share in Japan's imports (c.i.f.)	24	20
Direct investment		
Japan's share in outward U.S. investment	3	4
Japan's share in inward investment in the U.S.	1	9
U.S. share in outward Japanese investment	24	27
U.S. share in inward investment in Japan	60	54

Sources: United States Department of Commerce, Bureau of Economic Analysis, *Survey of Current Business* and *Statistical Abstract of the United States*; Ministry of Finance, *Okurasho Kokusai Kin'yukyoku Nenkan*; and Japan Economic Institute, *JEI Report.*

On the other hand, Japan does not occupy the center of American attention in the same way: the United States has other trading partners of close to equal importance. Since a large share of Japan's exports to the United States are consumer products, Americans are now much more aware of Japan and its economic success than they were in the 1960s, but a sense of need or importance is still missing. Politicians in Washington make statements to the effect that Japan exports nothing to the United States that we really need or could not produce ourselves. In a crude sense, that statement has some truth, but it seriously underestimates the economic value of Japan to the United States.

This unbalanced dependency may feed into relations around the region in two ways. First, the United States may press Japan harder on trade issues because it feels that less is at stake. This may have contributed to the rather negative and harsh tone in bilateral relations discussed earlier. Second, Japan realizes that it has little choice but to accede to U.S. demands. It must make concessions, however grudgingly, on opening Japanese markets of interest to the United States, and it must voluntarily restrain some exports to the United States. This necessity may also contribute to the rising amount of Japanese foreign direct investment flowing to the United States. Faced with protectionist threats, an increasing number of Japanese firms are moving manufacturing operations to the United States in order to protect their long-term position.

This dependency may affect Japan's relations with the rest of the region in a way best understood through reference to the hierarchical nature of Japanese society, in which truly equal relationships are relatively rare. Most people see themselves in a web of personal ties in which other people are either above or below them in some ill-defined social sense. A person looks up to his or her parents, older siblings, teachers, older fellow students and older fellow employees. Conversely, he or she will expect a certain amount of respect or deference from younger fellow students or employees, younger siblings, children and other younger relatives. Situations in which one can feel entirely equal with another person are relatively few, such as fellow students in the same class, or fellow employees who entered the firm in the same year and have not moved to a superior management position.

Economists should be very humble when treading into sociology, but a convincing argument can be made that the Japanese tend to see the rest of the world in the same hierarchical terms in which they view their own society. The world is composed of vertical relationships, with some contries in a superior position and others in an inferior position. "Superior" and "inferior" are intentionally left undefined here because they are vague feelings rather than clear concepts. In this international hierarchy, Japan has felt itself to be inferior to the United States in the postwar period. As an inferior, Japan expected protective, paternalistic treatment by the United States. Although Japan's rapid economic rise has brought its per capita income up to a level close to that of the United States, most Japanese still have a vague sense of inferiority. This is a difficult concept to deal with because many Japanese feel quite superior in terms of technology and have developed a considerable contempt for the United States. Nevertheless, in a broader sense they see the United States as bigger and stronger than Japan, both economically and militarily.

As an inferior in this bilateral relationship, Japan recognizes that it must make some concessions in bilateral negotiations. Since the U.S. market is so important, economic rationality alone implies that it would ill behoove the Japanese to behave in a manner that would jeopardize their access to it. But many people also reveal a sense of inferiority when they mention the necessity or inevitability of conceding to U.S. pressure.

The same sense of hierarchy can be applied to Japan's relations with other countries in Northeast Asia. All the others fall into the category of inferiors to Japan, at least in terms of per capita income levels. Feeling superior to those countries, the Japanese often see less necessity to make concessions when pressed, unless there are mitigating factors such as access to a vital raw material. Some Japanese display a strong attitude of arrogance and contempt toward these countries, which does not further smooth international relations. Since trade barriers of concern to developing countries have been declining in Japan, this problem may be more one of style than of substance.

Japanese concessions to the United States may come at the cost of a harder line against the requests of developing countries for removal of trade barriers. Opponents to change argue that the political system can be pushed only so far.

These problems all fall into a grey area, but the above interpretation is a reflection of attitudes revealed during the research mission. In addition, most of the other countries of the area appear to see the world in the same hierarchical terms as does Japan, accepting the idea that Japan is superior to them in an economic sense. One hesitates to make too much of this sociological point since these countries have harshly criticized Japan on economic issues at various times, but a willingness to accept Japan as a superior country did pervade many discussions.

Although the dominant U.S.-Japan relationship can make the resolution of trade problems more difficult for Japan's other trading partners, in another sense that relationship may be to their benefit. By virtue of size, strength and indispensability to Japan, the United States has been able to force Japan to lower import barriers to the benefit of all its trading partners. Were it not for the heavy pressure from the United States, the import barriers in Japan would likely be much higher than they are.

Where there is overlap on products of interest, the dominant position of the United States benefits other countries as well.

Describing the U.S.-Japan relationship as dominant and key to understanding the rest of the ties in the region runs counter to a common American perception of Japan's role in Asia. According to this alternative interpretation, Japan is best seen as an Asian country. With its cultural similarities and geographical proximity to the rest of Asia, Japan could sever or greatly curtail its economic ties with the United States and replace them with much closer ties to Asia. China often figures prominently in these statements, in visions of combining Japanese technology with Chinese manpower. This concept is based on the economic co-prosperity sphere that was part of Japanese ideology during the 1930s, and it is often painted in the same negative colors.

This alternative interpretation of Japan's options is unrealistic. The strength of Japan's dependency on the the U.S. market is so strong that a large-scale move away from it could not be managed without severe adjustment costs for Japan. Economic ties are not chess pieces that can be moved around on a playing board. The economic flows of goods, services and capital between Japan and the United States and between Japan and other Northeast Asian countries are determined largely by economic factors, and a rearrangement of those ties would not be easy or economically rational. Those forces have resulted in a strengthening of Japan's ties to the United States rather than a weakening over the past several years. If Japan's exports to the United States were severely constrained, it is not at all clear that they could be redirected to an Asian market. Conversely, if Japan chose to cut its imports from the United States, Asian countries would have great difficulty replacing them. Although there is some overlap in export structure, the developing countries do not produce many of the sophisticated products that Japan buys from the United States. Whether the role of the United States benefits or hinders the ability of other countries in the region to solve their own problems with Japan, the dominance of this particular bilateral tie stands out and does not appear to be replaceable by a stronger Japan-Asia tie.

V. The Newly Industrializing Countries

Although they are separated considerably by income levels and development strategy, South Korea, Taiwan and Hong Kong make a convenient subdivision of Northeast Asia with a number of elements in common. As seen from Table 1, these are the countries in the region with the highest growth performance over the past decade, ranging from 7.5 percent in South Korea and Taiwan to 9.3 percent in Hong Kong. Along with Singapore they are often referred to as the newly industrializing countries (NICs), or sometimes as the "four little dragons." Implicit in these terms is the assumption that they represent highly successful countries, rapidly moving up the industrial ladder in much the same way as did Japan in the 1950s and 1960s. In assessing their relationship with Japan, however, several features stand out: they are the most highly dependent on trade for the growth and development of their domestic economies; all face uncertainties in their economic future; Japan is important to them through a variety of economic ties, but somewhat less important than one might expect; economic ties with Japan appear to be weakening in relative terms over time rather than strengthening; and none of them is currently expressing the level of frustration with Japan that typifies reactions in Washington.

Trade Dependency

Table 10 demonstrates the relative openness of Northeast Asian countries to trade, using the ratio of exports to gross domestic product (GDP). Japan tends to be pictured as a trade-dependent country, but in terms of this ratio it is not. At 14 percent, the ratio of exports to GDP in Japan is only a little over double that of the United States, primarily because the U.S. ratio has slipped considerably in the 1980s as the strong value of the dollar hurt exports. The European countries, for example, all have export ratios that are considerably higher than Japan's. China, a large continental country, also has an export ratio that is in the range of Japan and the United States.

Compared to these rather modest levels, the export ratios of the three NICs vary from 35 percent for South Korea to 89 percent for Hong Kong. This latter value may not be realistic, since a large portion of Hong Kong's exports are simply reshipments of products coming from elsewhere (and especially from China). Even excluding reshipments, though, the export ratio for Hong Kong comes to 45 percent.

With such a large share of economic activity going to exports, fluctuations in export growth have a large impact on overall economic perform-

35

Table 10

Exposure to Trade

Country	Exports/GDP 1984
United States	6%
Japan (GNP)	14
South Korea	35
Taiwan	53
Hong Kong	89[a]
China	10

[a] 45% if reexports are excluded.

Source: International Monetary Fund, *International Financial Statistics Yearbook, 1985;* Council for Economic Planning and Development, Republic of China, *Taiwan Statistical Data Book,* 1985; and data from U.S. Consulate in Hong Kong.

ance. All other factors held constant, a jump in Taiwan's exports of 10 percent would lead to a 5 percent gain in GNP because the export ratio is just over 50 percent. In reality, the impact is not that large since GNP includes net exports (exports of goods and services minus imports). Every dollar of increased exports includes some amount of imports. Ships built in Korean shipyards, for example, generally use engines imported from Japan. On the other hand, every dollar of exports also has an impact on increasing plant and equipment investment by industries that produce exports, as well as the incomes (and eventual consumption spending) of the workers in those industries, adding to the initial impact of export growth. Therefore, the effect of export fluctuations on these economies is very large.

Not only are these three countries highly dependent on exports, but Japan and the United States are their largest single markets (see Table 5). For South Korea, these two markets together take 52 percent of its exports, while for Taiwan the level is 40 percent and for Hong Kong it is 38 percent. A 10 percent jump in Taiwan's exports to the United States alone, with all other factors held constant, would increase GNP by about 1.5 percent. This means that the rate of growth and changes in protectionism in Japan and the United States are questions of vital interest to these NICs.

Now the importance of the U.S.-Japan relationship becomes more clear. In 1984, for example, a year in which the Taiwanese economy (measured as real GDP) grew at the very high rate of 10.3 percent, the domestic components of Taiwan's economy grew slower: consumer spending was up 8.0 percent, government consumption 7.0 percent, and private-sector investment only 3.5 percent. On the other hand, exports of goods and services rose 18.9 percent and imports 13.3 percent to produce a jump in net exports of 52.8 percent. Fully 66 percent of the increase in total merchandise exports for 1984 was accounted for by the United States, and an additional 13.3 percent by Japan. Therefore, 80 percent of export growth was due to increased sales to Japan and the United States, which in turn pushed up the rate of overall economic growth. Conversely, 1985 will turn out to be a year of disappointing growth for Taiwan; when the data are finally announced, decelerating export expansion to the United States will undoubtedly turn out to be a major cause.

Over the long run, the openness to trade also demonstrates the danger to these countries of any protectionist spiral resulting from U.S.-Japan trade tension. The three NICs would be swept up in any general protectionist measures adopted by the United States, and more indirectly, the spillover from U.S.-Japan antagonism would certainly sour the reaction of the U.S. government to imports from these other countries.

Finally, the dependence on exports leads to doubts about the ability of these countries to achieve high rates of growth into the future. The current target for economic growth in Taiwan from 1985 to 2000 is 6.5 percent. For South Korea, the projection is approximately 8 percent over the same time period. Embedded in these projections are optimistic expectations about export growth. The South Korean forecast, for example, assumes that the nominal dollar value of its exports will grow at 15 percent until 1990 and at 14 percent thereafter. That forecast is somewhat below the actual performance of Korean exports over the decade from 1974 to 1983, when average annual growth in merchandise exports was 18 percent, but because the projection for the future assumes lower inflation, the real growth implied by these figures may not be very different.

Are these projections realistic? Small countries can expand their exports rapidly by gaining market share in foreign markets. This is especially true of developing countries because many of their exports, such as textiles and footware, are in product areas where global demand is not expanding rapidly, so that large gains can be made only at the expense of other producers. As long as the absolute amounts are relatively small, those gains may not be difficult to achieve. With two decades of rapid growth, however, the three NICs are much larger and the size of their exports much more significant than earlier. This creates two problems: competition from other producers may make further jumps in market share abroad difficult to achieve, and rapid increases are more likely to provoke protectionist responses. According to the theory of comparative advantage, these countries should increase their market share in product areas where they have comparative advantage, but once they have

37

achieved that shift, export growth may slow unless they can successfully develop new industries to repeat the process.

The expectation of continued rapid export expansion assumes that comparative advantage will lead to continued market share gains, and that those gains will not bring a protectionist response from the United States. That assumption may turn out to be correct, but it is certainly open to doubt.

During the research mission, scholars and officials in both Taiwan and South Korea acknowledged the problems inherent in their high dependence on exports. The next five-year economic plan in South Korea, for example, has as one of its basic goals development of a broader domestic market so that the ratio of exports to GNP will decline. Forecasts in Taiwan also expressed a goal of reducing dependence on exports through pursuit of an objective of "balanced" growth. Even with that objective supposedly embedded in official forecasts of economic growth, the expectations about export expansion sound highly optimistic.

Put in terms of simple economic theory, this consideration of the future involves the distinction between the efficient allocation of resources in the economy at any particular time and the allocation that is most efficient in producing growth and increased income in the future. Investment in export industries in which these countries have had comparative advantage has been a successful strategy to produce growth up until now, but continued heavy allocation of investment resources to these industries could lead to lower growth or recession in the future. They must now decide what new or different allocation of investment within the economy will prove to be the most efficient.

A related question is the ability of these economies to move production and exports to new industries where rapid export market share gains will again be possible. In both South Korea and Taiwan there is considerable concern about this issue, with a strong sense that the economies now face difficult turning points. Taiwanese officials are aware that the economy has done well in developing the labor-intensive industries in which the country's international comparative advantage lay, but that with rising income levels a shift is now needed into more sophisticated products. Over the past few years in Taiwan, private-sector investment in the plant and equipment necessary for the economy to grow and evolve has been lagging, which is evidence that business may be unable to bring about the necessary transition to less labor-intensive products. When I visited Taiwan, a government-sponsored commission had just completed a study of appropriate government policies to encourage and assist the shift, but the report was considered to be rather disappointing.

Future Uncertainty

Beyond the dangers implicit in being very exposed to trade, these three countries face other uncertainties that could have long-term implications for the economic development of the region. Anyone who sees Asia as a realistic alternative for Japan's close economic relationship with the United States should think carefully about these potential problems. None of these countries is characterized by the degree of stability and freedom from political dilemmas that Japan exhibited during its high-growth era.

South Korea lives under the constant threat of military invasion by North Korea, and both North and South believe that the country is artificially divided. Peaceful reunification is not possible in the forseeable future, but the situation is certainly not stable and could produce more terrorist actions like the bombing of the plane carrying South Korean cabinet members in Rangoon.

Driven by the belief that true democracy in the face of the military threat from North Korea is impossible, South Korea is characterized by a certain amount of political repression and faces difficulty in moving toward a more stable, open democratic system. It has not had a peaceful transfer of power from one leader to another in the postwar period, and whether such a transfer can be managed in the elections scheduled for 1988 remains to be seen. Faced with limitations on political expression, the opposition tends to become more militant, including periodic outbursts of student demonstrations. Japan also had its episodes of protest, but rarely with the degree of violence or hostility that appears in South Korea. The transfer of power from Chun Doo Hwan in 1988 through peaceful elections could conceivably occur as scheduled and lead to an era of strengthened democracy, but that outcome is by no means assured.

Taiwan has similar problems that make its future cloudy. Politically, the country has been very stable, without the violent changes in leadership that have characterized South Korea. However, Taiwan is saddled with a constitution and government that claim to represent all of China and can see no realistic way to change that situation. As absurd as that claim may be, perhaps the most dangerous move that Taiwan could make would be to rewrite the constitution and declare itself to be an independent country with no connection to China. That development would be more unpalatable and unacceptable to the government in Beijing than continuation of the present charade because it would eliminate the possibility of eventual reunification.

The trouble with the illusion of representing China is twofold. First, it puts constraints on political expression because the government cannot allow the opposition to advocate an independent Taiwan. This has led to

39

a certain amount of violence and repression in the political system, although it has remained at a relatively low level. Second, Taiwan has had great difficulty in dealing with the opening of China to trade with the rest of the world. Even though Taiwan does trade with China, the government cannot officially recognize or condone it. This could become an increasing problem for Taiwan as its businessmen will not want to be artificially constrained from free participation in an important regional market in which many of their international competitors are involved.

Hong Kong faces a more concrete problem. In 1997 ownership reverts to China. Arrangements for that transfer have involved elaborate agreements to ensure that after 1997 Hong Kong will be able to continue an existence not much different than it enjoys now. However, once the transfer takes place, what real guarantee is there that the Chinese government will not impose regulations that stifle the unique entrepreneurial character of Hong Kong? As discussed in other monographs in this series, a number of factors could constrain Chinese behavior, but no one can be positive of the outcome. At the present time, this uncertainty apparently has not affected economic activity. During the research visit, virtually everyone with whom I spoke pointed to the short time horizon for most investments; in an environment where people expect to get a return on their investment in three years, 1997 is not yet relevant. Only in the early 1990s, they said, would investors begin to worry about the future of Hong Kong and consider moving their money and businesses elsewhere.

While investors in Hong Kong are still unperturbed, anyone considering the long-term future of the region should give some thought to this issue. Hong Kong has been the most dynamic spot in the region over the past decade, and changes that damage its vitality would not be good either for Hong Kong or for China.

All three Northeast Asian NICs could manage their futures well. South Korea might see a peaceful election in 1988 and avoid military conflict with North Korea. Taiwan could continue to live indefinitely with its unrealistic constitution and find unofficial ways to allow trade with China to continue to expand. Hong Kong might continue its vigorous economic life under Chinese rule after 1997. But the future is not certain in the sense that political stability in Japan or the United States is certain.

For at least South Korea and Taiwan, economic growth appears to have helped keep the political problems in abeyance. With incomes rising rapidly, the majority of people have been willing to tolerate moderate infringements on political expression and repression of dissidents. Continued healthy economic growth may be a key element in their future political stability. In the absence of high growth, the broad toleration of the existing regimes could crumble. Thus, Japan and the United States, through their macroeconomic and trade policies, may hold the key to regional political stability as well as regional economic performance.

Japan could also face some difficulty if it were to follow a scenario of substituting closer ties with Asia for its current close economic ties with the United States. These three countries, at least, present a less certain economic picture than does the United States. They are growing much more rapidly, but what would happen to Japanese exports if a serious recession occurred in these countries? Even now that would have a negative effect on Japan, and a shift that made Japan more dependent on their markets would heighten the impact.

Dependence on Japan

In the previous section, the point was made that the economic ties of both Japan and the United States to the region are quite strong. But looking specifically at ties between the three NICs and Japan, the case can be made that they are somewhat weaker than might be expected given the geographical proximity and basic cultural similarities. In addition, some of these ties appear to be weakening over time rather than strengthening.

Japan is close to all of these countries. Separated by only one time zone (and none in the case of South Korea) and short air flights, Japanese businessmen have a great travel advantage over their American counterparts in conducting trade with these countries. In addition, there are strong common cultural threads in this societies based on their Sinitic heritage. Although Japan has a distinctive spoken language, it does use Chinese characters, which eases the cross-national language difficulties (although use of Chinese characters in South Korea is now very limited). In addition, since both South Korea and Taiwan have been Japanese colonies, people over the age of about fifty still have a good command of the Japanese language.

Other similar cultural aspects include a common Confucian orientation, Buddhism as a major religion, and various art forms. Such basic elements in common, however, should not be taken to mean that people behave in similar ways. Anyone who has spent time in Japan and the other countries can appreciate the large differences in behavior patterns.

Economic patterns could also point to a convenient fit between Japan and these other countries. As a recently industrialized nation, Japan is rapidly moving out of industries that the three NICs are entering. Textiles in Japan, for example, have been in rapid decline for the past two decades. Therefore, comparative advantage should lead to a comfortable fit, with Japan accepting labor-intensive products from these countries and exporting capital- and skill-intensive products to them.

41

All of the above reasons suggest that Japan ought to be the dominant trading partner for all three of the NICs in the region. The United States, as the major alternative trading partner, is much farther away, has no cultural affinity with any of the countries, and trains very few people in the local languages. But the data do not support this assumption. Turning back to Table 5, Japan outdistances the United States as a supplier of goods to these countries by only a small margin (except in the case of Hong Kong, where Japan's exports are twice as large). As a share of their imports, Japan represents 25–30 percent, a large position but roughly balanced by the United States. On the export side, the United States absorbs a far greater share than does Japan. Japan takes only 4 percent of Hong Kong's exports, 10 percent of Taiwan's, and 16 percent of South Korea's. The U.S. portion ranges from a quarter to a half of total exports from these countries.

Japan's role has also diminished somewhat over time, as demonstrated in Table 11. Japan's share in Taiwan's imports rose somewhat in the 1960s but then dropped considerably, from over 40 percent in 1970 to less than 30 percent in 1984. In contrast, since 1970 the U.S. share has been rather steady at 23 percent. The export side shows a much more dramatic shift, with Japan falling from 38 percent to 10 percent between 1960 and 1984 while the United States rose from 12 percent to 49 percent.

Table 11
Trade with the United States and Japan
(percentage of shares within total exports or imports)

	Imports		Exports	
	Japan	United States	Japan	United States
South Korea				
1960	41.2%	19.9%	63.7%	11.7%
1970	40.7	29.4	28.0	46.7
1984	24.8	22.6	15.9	36.3
Taiwan				
1960	35.3	38.1	37.7	11.5
1970	42.8	23.9	14.6	38.0
1984	29.3	23.0	10.5	48.8
Hong Kong				
1960	15.3	11.7	5.4	15.3
1970	23.8	13.2	7.1	35.6
1984	23.0	11.0	4.4	33.2

Note: Each percentage figure represents the share of the United States or Japan in global exports or imports for each country.
Source: International Monetary Fund, *Direction of Trade;* Council for Economic Planning and Development, Republic of China, *Taiwan Statistical Data Book.*

For South Korea, a similar change has taken place. Japan's role in Korean imports doubled from 20 percent in 1960 to around 40 percent in 1970 and then dropped back to 25 percent by 1984. On the export side as well, Japan's share has slipped from 64 percent in 1960 to 28 percent in 1970 and only 16 percent by 1984.

Only Hong Kong varies from this pattern. Japan's share in Hong Kong's imports has remained constant, at 23 percent between 1970 and 1984, but so has the U.S. share, dropping only from 13 percent to 11 percent. The U.S. share has been consistently lower than Japan's since 1960. On the export side, though, the United States has thoroughly dominated Hong Kong's exports. Since 1970, the United States has taken roughly 33 to 35 percent of Hong Kong's exports while Japan's share has sunk from 7 percent to only 4 percent.

These data can be interpreted as demonstrating Japan's importance to the region, but given its geographical and cultural proximity to the NICs, the data also reveal weaker economic ties than could be expected. Japan has burst upon the scene as an industrial power and a major world exporter in the past twenty years, but it has not displaced the United States as a trading partner for these three nations. If anything, the evidence shows some shift away from Japan toward the United States or the rest of the world.

One explanation for the declining role of Japan in the imports of Taiwan and South Korea is the rise in oil prices. As the oil import bill for both of these countries rose after 1973, the share of imports from OPEC rose and those from all other countries fell. But this does not provide a complete explanation. Rising oil prices do not explain the greater drop in the share of imports from Japan than from the United States, with the U.S. role relatively constant after 1970 in Taiwan and falling much less rapidly in the case of South Korea. In addition, a closer look at annual data in the case of Taiwan shows that Japan's share was rising while that of the United States was falling during the 1950s and 1960s, but that long-term trend stopped in the 1970s. Individual years show some minor variations, but the share of imports from Japan has been roughly constant since the mid-1970s. In the case of Korea, Japan's share in total imports continued to drop after the oil shocks, whereas the U.S. share did not.

A partial explanation for these trends was suggested at meetings in Taiwan and South Korea during the research mission. Put concisely, these countries do not want to be heavily dependent on Japan, and they have deliberately tried to move away from that dependency. In Taiwan, specific mention was made of the deliberate and desirable strategy of decreasing dependence on imports from Japan. Concern was also expressed that Taiwan has faced increasing problems in exporting to Japan as Taiwan's export structure has shifted away from raw materials and agricultural products toward manufactures over the past two decades. Playing on the competition between Japan and the United States, suggestions were even made that the United States ought to invest more in Taiwan as a low-wage manufacturing base from which to compete with Japanese companies in world markets.

In South Korea, a somewhat different concern brought up at our meetings was that Korean exports include a high level of imported parts from Japan. The problem lies in inadequate development of domestic parts supply for major export industries. Officials from the Ministry of Trade and Industry stated that progress is being made in this direction. As emphasis on developing a better domestic infrastructure of light industry bears fruit, the outcome could be reduced reliance on imports from Japan, although there might be an equal impact on imports from the United States.

Only in Hong Kong did there appear to be little concern or thought over the role of Japan in imports and exports. One explanation is the fierce belief in laissez faire: free of artificial barriers to trade, officials in Hong Kong believe in letting economic forces determine the nature of foreign trade ties. In addition, Hong Kong has never been as dependent as Taiwan and Korea on Japan as a source of imports, and its dependence has remained steady at just under one-quarter of all imports since 1970. Japan is also a far less important export market.

Given the awareness in Taiwan and South Korea of economic dependence on Japan, any large restructuring of relationships in the region involving closer ties with Japan and weaker ties with the United States appears unlikely. Further progress in import substitution in both countries might actually lead to a further decline in dependence on Japan.

Official Economic Relations with Japan

With two of the three NICs in Northeast Asia desiring to reduce the relative importance of Japan in their imports, and all three of them facing sizable trade imbalances with Japan, frustration and anger would be understandable. At various times in the past, in fact, both Taiwan and South Korea have been very vocal in their criticisms of Japan. However, one of the surprising findings of the research mission was the muted level of criticism or antagonism expressed.

In South Korea, bilateral relations with Japan were characterized as the best in the entire postwar period. Considering that the Koreans look back with great bitterness upon their experience as a colonial possession of Japan in the first half of the twentieth century and were not able to work out a treaty to normalize relations after the war until 1965, this is a significant development. A number of factors have contributed to the improving tone of relations, including Prime Minister Nakasone's trip to South Korea and President Chun Doo Hwan's trip to Japan, the first exchange of official state visits in the postwar period. The conclusion of antagonistic negotiations over a $6 billion foreign aid demand by South Korea which resulted in the 1983 announcement of a multiyear $4 billion package, may also have cleared the atmosphere. During meetings in Seoul, it was also pointed out that the hard-line approach in trade negotiations did not seem to work very well.

Illustrating the positive tone of economic relations, bilateral discussions at the end of 1985 produced routine results. While acknowledging the bilateral trade imbalance and problems of access to the Japanese market, participants also emphasized noncontroversial actions like Korean product fairs in Japan.

Taiwan fits the same pattern as South Korea. In a pique of anger several years ago, Taiwan temporarily banned a long list of Japanese products, but that move was quickly rescinded after domestic protests, and no return to such strident actions appears likely. In both Taiwan and South Korea, people had to be pressed to say anything about trade barriers in Japan. Most comments about the difficulty of exporting to Japan concerned the demanding nature of the Japanese market and the need to upgrade product quality in order to penetrate it. This should not be taken to mean that criticism of Japan has completely disappeared; while I was in Taipei, local newspapers were carrying stories about particular problems with Japan, such as allegations of danger resulting from the allocation of older planes to the subsidiary of Japan Air Lines that flies to Taipei, and rumors that Japanese trading companies falsify their accounts to hide profits in Taiwan in order to avoid taxes. Such problems, however, appear to have a very low priority among the government officials, businessmen and scholars with whom I spoke.

Such a small portion of Hong Kong's exports go to Japan that little interest was expressed there. It is surprising that the NIC that is the most dependent on exports and that exports so little to Japan, does not criticize Japan more heavily or try to break down the barriers to its exports. No such attitude was expressed in any of my meetings. International economic attention in Hong Kong does not seem to be directed toward Japan.

Compared to the frustration expressed almost daily in Washington, all of these countries gave a very quiet impression in the fall of 1985. In fact, in all three, far more attention was directed to problems with the United States, since Congress was considering further restrictions on textile imports, and the administration had initiated a series of trade cases against products from these countries to demonstrate to Congress its resolve to "do something" about trade problems.

The sense of international hierarchy provides at least one explanation for this relative calm. Both South Korea and Taiwan look up to Japan in some sense, and this may mute their objections to some Japanese policies. Another factor is that both countries are now under international pressure to liberalize their own import barriers. They can no longer complain loudly about Japan without taking some actions of their own.

Summary

South Korea, Taiwan and Hong Kong are different from one another, but they can still be usefully grouped together. As the three NICs in Northeast Asia, they share strong economic growth rates and a high degree of dependence on foreign trade. Japan has been important for their economic development and will undoubtedly continue to be important in the future. Despite the emphasis here on problems, it is well to reiterate that this has been a very positive role overall, the outcome of mutually beneficial economic interactions.

Two features of these relationships stand out. First, the United States has by no means been excluded from the region as Japan has grown economically stronger. The role of Japan, while very strong, appears to be somewhat smaller than one might think given geographical and cultural affinity. Second, the prospects for a future Japanese shift away from its close economic ties with the United States and toward a tighter set of relationships in Asia appears very unlikely. Even though most of the people interviewed during the research mission in these countries did not express any strong criticism of Japan, they also emphasized their import substitution strategies and the trend of declining dependence on Japan. They all appear unwilling to see Japan assume a much stronger economic role in the region, especially if it implies weakening ties with the United States. A strong but balanced dependence on both countries is probably a very good strategy because they can use the competition between the two to their own benefit.

VI. China

China forms another subdivision of Northeast Asia. It is a socialist country that has recently undergone extensive reforms, including much greater openness in its external economic ties. Having fought two wars with Japan within the past century, China also has ample reason to distrust the Japanese. But tempering that natural reaction has been the surprising degree of pragmatism embodied in the policies of the past few years. Perhaps it is still too early to assess the future course of the Chinese economy and its foreign economic relations because the reforms are not yet completed, but certain features do stand out. Among the striking aspects of the bilateral relationship with Japan are a resemblance to the position of the three Northeast Asian NICs on many issues; the strong visible economic ties that have developed rather quickly; the ability of China to balance or control the relationship; and the effect of uncertainties over the future on the interest of Japanese companies in dealing with China.

Similarities to NICs

Embarking on a series of economic reforms since 1978, China has developed many of its external economic relations in a manner similar to those of South Korea, Taiwan and Hong Kong. China is a large continental nation, and economists find that such countries tend to have relatively low exposure to international trade. The ratio of exports to GNP for China is much lower than in any of the NICs, but the policy of opening to the rest of the world has brought a rapid expansion of trade, to the point where exports are estimated to be about 10 percent of GNP, a level actually higher than in the United States.

In addition to being relatively open to trade given its size, China displays a striking degree of pragmatism in attitudes and policies on external economic matters. Even though it is a communist system, the economic topics and discussions at my meetings in Beijing more closely resembled those in the NICs than those in Moscow. Emphasis was on what would work and how to pay for it. Although ideology was not entirely absent, and in some cases Chinese reactions were puzzling until viewed in the context of their basic ideological framework, it did seem to play a less important role than in the Soviet Union on foreign economic issues. China gives the appearance of having adopted economic development as a national goal; like the NICs, it is willing to turn to any and all external sources for assistance in that process. This attitude means that China has quickly become involved in and integrated with the region.

47

Given the practicality of its outward strategy, China has found that Japan is a valuable source of technology, capital (in the form of both direct investment and loans), and manufactured imports (especially investment goods). In addition, China must confront its trade imbalances with Japan and find ways to cope with them. These issues are considered below.

Stronger Ties with Japan

Japan is the largest export destination and source of imports for China other than Hong Kong, and much of the trade with Hong Kong is simply passed through to the rest of the world (see Table 5). For both exports and imports, the relationship with Japan is approximately twice as large as with the United States. None of the three NICs just discussed has a trade relationship that is so much more dependent on Japan than the United States. The percentage share of total exports that goes to Japan is also higher than for any of the NICs.

Not only are the trade ties strong, but they are very visible. On street corners in Beijing where patriotic slogans were displayed just a few years ago, billboards now carry advertisements for Japanese consumer appliances. A recent large purchase has meant that now most of the Beijing taxi fleet is composed of Toyotas. Japanese vehicles are also heavily represented among trucks, buses and small vans. Japanese refrigerators and other appliances being delivered on bicycles are not an uncommon sight in Beijing. The Japanese material presence is thus highly visible.

During the summer prior to the research mission, Chinese students demonstrated against Japan, ostensibly over the visit of Prime Minister Nakasone to the Yasukuni Shrine in Tokyo, the burial site of Japanese soldiers, including a number of prominent figures found guilty at the war crimes trials. However, some Chinese described the motives as being broader, reflecting resentment over Japan's visible material presence in China. If true, this reaction is similar to what occurred in Thailand and other Southeast Asian countries in the early 1970s as Japanese products became more prominent. It would not be at all surprising if the student protest did encompass a sense of distaste for the recent "invasion" from Japan. Although Japanese companies could be criticized for their eager, aggressive promotion of their products, such protests are not likely to have any lasting importance.

In contrast to the strong trade ties, comments were made repeatedly in both Tokyo and Beijing about the relative lack of Japanese direct investment in China. This investment has lagged behind that by American firms. The Chinese have complained about the relatively low investment by the Japanese, but it is not clear if the "problem" should be accepted at face value. First, investment in any form by foreign companies in China is a very recent phenomenon; thus, the present pattern may be completely changed in a few years as more investment takes place. Second, the bulk of U.S. investment is in oil exploration, an area where Japan has never had a strong international position. If oil investment is excluded, Japan no longer ranks so far behind. Third, focus on *direct* investment can be very misleading. Even though Japanese firms may not be involved in joint ventures owning factories, Japan has played an important role in lending to China. For example, two of the four foreign bond issues made by the China International Trust and Investment Corporation (CITIC) were in Japan and accounted for about half of the funds raised. Japanese data indicate a total of ¥115 billion (roughly $500 million at then-current exchange rates) in bonds issued by various Chinese agencies in Japan as of March 1985. According to one Chinese official, if lending is added to direct investment activity, Japan is providing more capital to China than is the United States.

In all, the economic ties between China and Japan are quite strong. Chinese complaints should be placed into context: the demonstrations over the Nakasone visit to the Yasukuni Shrine and the vocal dissatisfaction over the low level of direct investment become bargaining points in bilateral discussions.

Balancing the Relationship

The second striking feature of Japan's economic relationship with China is the continued ability of the Chinese government to control the outcomes. Unlike the capitalist economies of the other countries in the region, the Chinese government still has firm control over external economic relations, although the recent reforms may eventually lead to a considerable erosion of that control. If the government perceives that its trade deficit has gotten out of control, it can simply cut imports by administrative decision. That option is not available to market economies.

One of the implications of the heavy government control over trade may be that China has a better bargaining position with Japan. Over the past two to three years, China has had a small but rapidly growing trade deficit with Japan. Officials with whom I spoke repeatedly expressed concern over a jump in the bilateral deficit from $1.2 billion in 1984 to $2.3 billion in the first six months of 1985. To combat this imbalance, the Chinese want to export more light manufactured goods to Japan, but they feel that they face problems from import barriers and established industrial structures in Japan. When negotiating these problems with the Japanese government, they can hold out the carrot of expanded Japanese exports to China, or the threat of cutting those sales if the trade imbalance worsens.

The previous section pointed out that the NICs seem to be at a disad-

49

vantage in dealing with Japan because of the dominance of the U.S.-Japan relationship. China may have escaped some of this disadvantage because of its control over trade. The NICs were also described as basically accepting the Japanese concept of international hierarchy, which limits their ability to obtain favorable action on their trade complaints. The Chinese do not seem to be affected as much by this; they are willing to respect economic Japan but feel no inferiority. In a historical setting, it is the Chinese who feel superior.

In addition to keeping the trade imbalances from getting too large, China appears to desire to balance the strength of its economic ties with other countries. It would be surprising, for example, if Japan's share in total Chinese imports continued to rise substantially. Although this was never stated as an explicit policy, many of the statements made during the research mission could be interpreted along these lines. Japan is a valuable economic partner, but the Chinese do not want to be overly dependent on it, and the government is able to regulate the geographical distribution of trade.

One might expect from these comments that China would be pressing very hard to get trade barriers in Japan reduced. Since it must move its export structure away from raw materials, the incentive for engaging in tough negotiations would appear to be amplified. However, just as with the three NICs, the attitudes expressed by a wide variety of officials during the research mission were surprisingly mild. Rather than complaining bitterly about barriers in Japan as do Americans, they pointed to problems of quality control and existing industrial structure. Since Japan has evolved as a nation that imports raw materials and produces most of the manufactured products it needs from those raw materials, there is little room for manufactured imports. Therefore, according to this line of reasoning, the solution is not the removal of trade barriers but an effort by Japan to change its industrial structure. This position reflects an admirable degree of realistic understanding of economic Japan, but room for complaint certainly remains.

In the absence of trade barriers, the principle of comparative advantage explained in the introduction implies that imports from countries like China should be rapidly replacing domestic Japanese products in labor-intensive industries. That is, the competitive pressure from abroad should bring about the change in Japan's industrial structure that the Chinese want to see occur. If that change is not taking place, or is taking place more slowly than the Chinese believe it should, then they ought to be pressing complaints about trade barriers that have impeded the process. As pointed out earlier, Japan has made considerable progress in lowering import barriers, but the process remains incomplete.

When pressed on the question of negotiating with Japan over the removal or lowering of import barriers, the Chinese expressed no anger

50

or frustration. Although this may have reflected the timing of the research mission, a reticence to discuss the issue, or simply the selection of people who were part of the discussions, the lack of criticism was particularly striking. Minister of Foreign Economic Relations and Trade Zheng Tuobin was reported at the end of November to be blaming the bilateral imbalance with Japan on the existence of import barriers, but even his criticism sounded very mild. His statement was replete with references to "friendship," "understanding," and "working together" with Japan as elements of a solution to the problem.

Uncertainties

China's economic relations with Japan are quite strong and have been growing at a rapid rate, as outlined above. Just as with the three Northeast Asian NICs, though, the future presents a number of uncertainties that ought to temper excessive enthusiasm (or fears) about the bilateral relationship.

The first cause for caution is the structure of Chinese exports to Japan. Earlier it was pointed out that countries need not (and in most cases should not) have balanced trade with each individual trading partner. However, given the fairly tight administrative control that China has over its foreign trade, and given its dilemma of exporting enough globally to pay for its imports, there is a focus on bilateral balances with countries like Japan. As long as that concern remains, the expansion of trade with Japan will be constrained by China's ability to export more to the Japanese market. The prospects are not very encouraging.

Table 12 presents data on the structure of Japan's imports from China. As is clearly evident, the bulk of those imports are raw materials, of which crude petroleum alone accounts for 39 percent (48 percent if refined products are included). The total of all raw materials (foodstuffs, textile fibers, metal ores and scrap, other materials and mineral fuels) comes to 76 percent. Of manufactured products, the main import is textiles (15 percent). Unless this structure changes, China will face a dilemma in expanding its exports to Japan. The slower economic growth in Japan explained earlier means that demand for many of these basic raw materials is also expanding relatively slowly, and for some, like petroleum, consumption has been stagnant or falling. Imports of crude petroleum have been dropping in volume since 1979, falling 24 percent by 1984. Compounding this problem has been the decline in world prices for petroleum and other raw materials.

The only hope for more rapid expansion of raw material exports would come from substitution of Chinese materials in place of those from other countries. The data in Table 12 indicate that for most of these products China represents a rather small share of total Japanese imports, which suggests ample room for such substitution. But even here there

51

Table 12
Imports from China, 1984

Item	Value $ millions	Share in Imports from China	Share in Japanese Global Imports
Foodstuffs	$ 630.3	10.6%	3.9%
Textile fibers	286.4	4.8	11.5
Metal ores and scrap	9.7	0.2	0.1
Other raw materials	503.9	8.4	4.8
(Wood)	(13.1)	(0.2)	(0.4)
Mineral fuels	3,093.1	51.9	5.1
(Coal)	(204.3)	(3.4)	(3.8)
(Crude petroleum)	(2,344.8)	(39.4)	(6.0)
(Petroleum products)	(542.7)	(9.1)	(8.9)
Chemicals	247.8	4.2	3.0
Machinery & equipment	14.7	0.2	0.1
Other	1,171.9	19.7	0.4
(Textile products)	(888.0)	(14.9)	(22.9)
(Nonferrous metals)	(32.3)	(0.5)	(0.7)
Total	$5,957.6	100.0%	4.4%

Source: Japan Tariff Association, *Trade Summary Report of Japan* (December 1984).

are problems, such as the fact that Chinese oil is very heavy crude that requires modification of Japanese refineries before it can be handled. In addition, since Japanese firms tend to import raw materials through long-term contracts, shifting suppliers can be difficult. Because total Japanese demand is stagnant, producers in all supplier countries are struggling to keep or expand their share in Japan's imports.

Given the difficulty in expanding raw material exports, China must turn to manufactured products, of which textiles offers the greatest promise. From 1978 through 1984, textile product exports to Japan expanded at an average annual rate of 19 percent (including a 51 percent increase in 1984). But Chinese competition, including that in textiles, comes at the labor-intensive end of the product scale, and at a time of slower economic growth in Japan there may be intensified opposition from small Japanese firms. Therefore, a shift toward a greater proportion of manufactures may embroil China in conflict with Japan over import barriers.

The second problem lies in the future course of economic reform in China. Agricultural reform has been thorough and successful, but industrial reforms will take longer and present many difficulties. The reform may succeed, but the process could at least be subject to periodic setbacks. This affects economic relations with Japan because the Japanese do not like uncertainty. Both the cutback in major construction projects in which Japanese firms were involved at the end of the 1970s and the failure to meet export commitments on oil have made the Japanese much more cautious in their dealings.

Third, uncertainty is reinforced by the unfinished institutional structure governing direct investment. Both Japan and the United States are still trying to negotiate treaties with China on direct investment, and Japanese firms may be somewhat less willing to become involved in China in the absence of such a treaty than are American firms. At stake in these negotiations are issues such as the conditions for repatriation of profits, national treatment (especially whether or not wages will be higher than in Chinese factories), compensation in case of changes in Chinese policies (that is, in case companies are nationalized), and the scope of disputes that could be referred to international arbitration. The Japanese are also unhappy over the Chinese desire to use joint ventures with foreign firms to produce exports, and thereby increase its foreign exchange earnings, while not permitting them to sell their output in the Chinese market. Japanese firms are much less interested in China as a low-wage base to remain competitive in world export markets than they are in local production as a means to sell products in China.

A final problem underlying the relationship is the Japanese concern over what they call the "boomerang" effect. The Chinese want to acquire technology from abroad to increase productivity, leapfrogging in much the same way as Japan did during its rapid growth era. The

Japanese are unwilling to transfer technology that could result in future competition from China, having as evidence their own emergence as the main competitors for the American firms from which they obtained technology in the past. This problem was mentioned often in our discussions, but perhaps it should not be taken entirely at face value. Technology *is* flowing from Japan to China—the Japanese complain that often the Chinese are not equipped to understand or use efficiently the technology that they want—and what is not obtainable from one firm may be obtainable from another.

The central point to these problems is the uncertainty surrounding economic reform in China and Japanese caution in the face of that uncertainty. The possibility of failure or reversal may impede investment, while the possibility of success may impede technology transfer. This has not prevented a rapidly expanding trade and investment relationship, but it may continue to hold investment activity and technology licensing contracts below levels that the Chinese desire.

Summary

China has some parallels to the NICs in Northeast Asia, although it has emerged on the international scene much more recently. In the space of just a few years since the major reforms began in 1978, Japan has forged a strong economic relationship with China, encompassing trade, direct investment, loans, foreign aid and technology transfer. That role has contributed to China's development goals and has made the two nations relatively satisfied with their bilateral relationship.

No one should conclude that this smooth tie implies the coming of a China-Japan economic combination that will dominate regional or world markets. The idea of Japanese technology and organization and cheap Chinese labor sounds threatening to some Americans, but it has little basis in reality. Japanese firms see opportunity in China, but they are tempered by a considerable amount of caution and concern that China could become a future competitor. At the very least, much time will pass before income levels in China rise to the point where demand for the consumer products at which Japan excels rises to a high level. The relationship will also be constrained by China's ability to expand exports to Japan, and by its desire to maintain a balance in all its external relationships.

For all these reasons, a Japan-China economic axis appears unlikely. The opening of China to trade with the West has allowed comparative advantage to work, benefitting all of China's trading partners, including the United States and Japan. The gains will continue to grow if the advanced countries are willing to accept the structural adjustments — letting labor-intensive industries continue to decline — that are necessary to accommodate China in the world trading system.

VII. The Soviet Bloc

Japan's economic ties with the Soviet bloc nations in Northeast Asia — the Soviet Union, Mongolia and North Korea — provide a stark contrast to those with other countries. The ties are extremely thin, are not expanding and developing, and face serious problems into the future. On the other hand, the rise of Mikhail Gorbachev to power in the Soviet Union may yet hail a new era of openness to the West. Because officials were uncertain about future policy, or had not yet been affected by the changes, the answers to our questions may have been biased or unrepresentative of future trends.

Thinness of Ties

After looking at the large role that Japan plays in the external ties of all other nations of Northeast Asia, the very limited relationship with the Soviet Union and its two close allies in the region is very striking, whether viewed from the Japanese or the Soviet perspective.

Table 5 indicates that neither Japan nor the United States is the largest partner for the nonbloc trade of the Soviet Union. These data, estimated by compiling the figures reported by other countries rather than directly from Soviet data (and thereby excluding trade with most other communist countries), show that Western Europe dominates trade. Both West Germany and Italy have stronger import and export ties with the Soviet Union than do Japan and the United States. In 1984, Japan accounted for only 4 percent of Soviet exports to the West and 7 percent of its imports. These figures would be far smaller if Soviet trade with other bloc nations were included in the totals. This illustrates an important point that will be amplified below: even though the Soviet Union is both a European and Asian nation by virtue of geography, its economic and intellectual ties are very strongly European.

From the Japanese side the ties are equally weak. Only 1.5 percent of Japan's exports in 1984 were destined for the Soviet Union, and only 1.0 percent came from the Soviet Union. These figures place this bilateral tie well below the volume of Japan's trade with China. Not only are the flows rather small, but they have been stagnant or falling over the past several years. Imports from the Soviet Union peaked at $2.0 billion in 1981 and then fell by 31 percent to only $1.4 billion in 1984, a level no higher than 1974. Exports to the Soviet Union similarly peaked at $3.6 billion in 1981 and then also fell by 31 percent to $2.5 billion in 1984, returning them to the level of 1978. Thus, trade with the Soviet Union has languished as Japan has continued to rise as an advanced industrial exporter of sophisticated products to the rest of the world.

If trade ties with the Soviet Union appear small, those with Mongolia and North Korea are virtually nonexistent. A small, landlocked nation wedged between China and the Soviet Union, Mongolia has very little trade outside of the Soviet bloc. In 1983, 97 percent of Mongolian exports were to the Soviet bloc, 2.3 percent went to other socialist countries (China), and only 0.6 percent went to capitalist countries. Only 1.5 percent of all imports came from capitalist countries. From the Japanese perspective, trade with Mongolia is so insignificant that it does not even appear in summary trade statistics.

North Korea is also an insignificant trading partner of Japan, providing only 0.1 percent of Japan's imports and absorbing only 0.2 percent of Japan's exports. By way of contrast, Japan's imports from North Korea are only 4 percent the size of imports from South Korea, and exports to North Korea are only 5 percent of those to South Korea.

Investment ties are equally weak. Japanese official data on foreign direct investment show no investments in either Mongolia or North Korea. Japanese statistics show six separate investments in the Soviet Union as of the end of 1983, amounting to only 0.6 percent of total Japanese foreign direct investment. This does not mean that these particular investments have not been important from the Soviet standpoint as a means to increase output or acquire technology in the particular industries involved, but the overwhelming size of Japan's investment ties with the rest of the world relative to those with the Soviet Union says a great deal.

For North Korea, both trade and investment are handicapped by an additional problem. In the early 1970s, North Korea borrowed heavily from countries like Japan and then defaulted on its loans. Efforts to reschedule those loans have not resulted yet in any serious action by North Korea to redeem its international credibility. Those defaulted loans form a critical block to expanded economic ties with North Korea.

The Dominance of Ideology

In every discussion in Moscow, ideology was a dominant presence shaping the views of Soviet scholars and officials toward their relationship with Japan. It was far stronger than in Beijing, where officials exhibited a much greater willingness to ignore the ideological aspects of increased ties with Japan and focus on the practicalities of trade and investment. Since ideological positions can change, and may be changing under Gorbachev's leadership, it is difficult to sort out what might happen in the future.

To summarize the Soviet view briefly, they seemed to have difficulty accepting Japan as a major world economic power. One person explained that Japan was not a technological leader because it has no extensive space program (and especially no manned space program), no nuclear weapons and no arms industry, the most important symbols of modern technology. Another jokingly described Japan as a "cockroach" nation, living off the technological crumbs dropped by the advanced nations, achieving a certain amount of economic success through the application of these technologies but hardly deserving of respect as an advanced nation. Officials at Gosplan bridled at the idea that they could use Japanese financial or technological cooperation in developing Siberian resources. None of the people with whom I met are responsible for actual decisions on trading with Japan or attempts to acquire Japanese technology, which may explain part of their contempt, but the fact remains that the attitudes expressed were completely at odds with those in discussions in all other nations of the region.

Also affecting attitudes toward economic Japan are other political considerations. The Soviets described Japan as a nation fully subservient to the wishes of the United States. In their view, the problems in the relationship are all on the side of Japan. Since the Japanese do not see their trade with the Soviet Union as vital, they were willing to sacrifice it to support the United States in the sanctions imposed after the invasion of Afghanistan. The large drop in two-way trade between Japan and the Soviet Union, however, cannot be explained entirely by tightening of restrictions on permissible exports imposed after 1980. More importantly, the willingness of Japan to allow American troops to be stationed on its soil and to follow the United States in basic diplomatic policies toward the Soviet Union is both a serious irritant to the Soviet Union and a further cause for contempt. It would not be too much of an exaggeration to say that the Soviets view the Japanese relationship with the United States as being on a par with the Eastern European relationship to the Soviet Union.

Even if the focus is on developments in the Japanese economy, the difference in perspective between the Soviets and other countries is striking. When asked about their view of the most important current developments in the Japanese economy, people in the other countries focused on probable growth rates and the effect on imports of likely changes in Japanese industrial structure. In Moscow, this dialogue began with a long discussion of the impact of industrial robots on the labor force in Japan, emphasizing the probability of increased labor problems. From a Marxist economic perspective, this question may be central, but it was topic of discussion unique to the Soviet Union.

As stated above, many of these attitudes could simply be a product of the official position on Japan. Foreign policy was very much in a state of flux in the fall of 1985, and ministerial-level talks resumed after an eight year break only in January 1986, with the visit of the Soviet foreign

Table 13

Imports from the Soviet Union, 1984

Item	Value $ millions	Share in Imports from Soviet Union	Share in Japanese Global Imports
Foodstuffs	$ 116.1	8.3%	0.7%
Textile fibers	84.3	6.0	3.4
Metal ores and scrap	37.1	2.7	0.6
Other raw materials	386.1	27.7	3.7
(Wood)	(356.1)	(25.5)	(9.1)
Mineral fuels	276.4	19.8	0.5
(Coal)	(118.7)	(8.5)	(2.2)
(Crude petroleum)	(16.3)	(1.2)	(0.0)
(Petroleum products)	(140.8)	(10.1)	(2.3)
Chemicals	43.5	3.1	0.5
Machinery & equipment	12.0	0.9	0.1
Other	438.3	31.4	2.2
(Textile products)	(0.1)	(0.0)	(0.0)
(Nonferrous metals)	(283.2)	(20.3)	(6.0)
Total	$1,394.0	100.0%	1.0%

Source: Japan Tariff Association, *Trade Summary Report of Japan* (December 1984).

minister to Tokyo. If the trend toward less confrontation and greater openness continues, the official or acceptable positions and attitudes on a wide variety of questions related to Japan could change. Recent press reports, for example, indicate that Gosplan has unveiled a list of fourteen areas in which it wants to seek technology from Japan, and in 1986 a fair displaying Japanese industrial goods will be held in Moscow. Nevertheless, one should be skeptical of a large change. The basic European orientation that seemed evident in Soviet thinking, coupled perhaps with a dose of racism, is likely to keep Japan from receiving the degree of respect and attention as an economic entity that is visible throughout the rest of the region.

Future Problems

If the Gorbachev reforms continue, the possibility of expanded trade, investment, and technology ties with Japan becomes stronger. Even a 40 percent increase in Japanese exports, though, would only bring the relationship back to where it was in 1981. What are the prospects for an expansion of trade back to or beyond that level?

The first problem lies in the Soviet export structure. From their perspective, any large expansion of imports from Japan must be accompanied by increased exports. As pointed out in the case of China, this is not necessary because in economic theory bilateral trade balances do not matter, but the issue was always put in this way during the discussions. Table 13 provides the same detail on Soviet exports to Japan as was provided in Table 12 for China. Approximately two-thirds of those exports are raw materials, with timber alone accounting for 26 percent. Although the Soviets appear to be somewhat more successful in exporting miscellaneous manufactured products (mostly nonferrous metal products) than the Chinese, the same problem concerning increased exports exists. None of the people involved in the discussions in Moscow even mentioned the possibility of increasing exports of manufactured products, which probably reflects a healthy realism about the quality of those products. On the other hand, they were uniformly pessimistic over the prospects for exporting larger amounts of raw materials. They pointed out, for example, that advanced timber-loading facilities in the Pacific port city of Nahodka are underutilized because timber exports to Japan have declined. Several people also realistically pointed out that with Japan's slower growth and changing industrial structure, its overall demand for raw materials will grow slowly at best.

Table 13 further reveals that the Soviet Union supplies rather small percentages of Japan's imports of raw materials, opening the possibility of expanded exports through larger market shares. But the prospect of substituting Soviet supplies for those from other nations is limited, for the same reasons pointed out for China. In addition, raw material exports to Japan are from Siberia, which has a harsh climate that makes the extraction of resources expensive. For oil, gas, and coal many of the deposits are also located far from the sea, so that high land-transportation costs also make these resources less attractive. Therefore, Siberian resources may not be price competitive in the current environment of falling world commodity prices.

As if the economic difficulties were not enough, political problems arise as well. Over the past decade, the Soviet Union has repeatedly acted in a way to raise Japanese concerns, including the buildup of Pacific naval forces and the downing of the Korean Airlines passenger plane. Petroleum resources in Siberia could also be used to fuel the Soviet military machine in the region, a prospect that does not appeal to the Japanese. In the short run, an improved atmosphere is unlikely to bring much change in Japanese mistrust of Soviet intentions.

All of these reasons suggest that an upturn in trade resulting from improving diplomatic relations will be moderate. Soviet attitudes toward Japan might change, but other economic and political constraints will remain operative. Two things would change this picture: a return to rapidly rising world commodity prices that would make the Japanese interested once again in Siberian resources, or a willingness on the part of the Soviets to make Japanese participation in Siberia more profitable. At present, neither of these eventualities appears likely.

VIII. Summary and Implications

Japan's economic impact on the countries of Northeast Asia is quite large in all cases except the Soviet bloc. Economists view international economic ties through trade, investment and technology as beneficial because they allow the scarce economic resources of the world to be put to the most productive use to the mutual benefit of all countries concerned. Japan's rapid industrialization and growing ties in the region have helped that process take place. Nonetheless, the purely economic gains from this relationship have been accompanied by a number of serious political problems.

From an American perspective, Japan has been increasingly viewed as an economic threat or as unfair in its trading practices. Complaints about trade problems have dominated the bilateral agenda and have raised the real prospect of retaliatory protectionist action by the United States. Even though broad protectionist moves have not materialized, the possibility has become stronger. Economists do not support an increase in protectionism because that would remove the gains achieved in the postwar period through allowing the principle of comparative advantage to work. The result would be stagnation or recession. A basic element of American frustration has been the belief that Japan has not done enough to uphold its end of the postwar liberal trade system. This has led to the incongruous result that we could become more protectionist because we want Japan to become less protectionist. The Japanese feel that they are being singled out unfairly by the United States, but the key to the future existence of the liberal trade system appears to lie with Japan and its actions to reduce import barriers.

The review of Japan's relations with other Northeast Asian countries has revealed that the frustration over Japan, so visible in the United States, does not characterize other countries at the present time. Whether because of hierarchical deference or greater realism, neither the Northeast Asian NICs nor China have joined the United States in heavy criticism of Japan. They have had problems with Japan, and were willing to express them when specifically asked, but the tone was quite subdued and mild. In fact, fears about protectionist moves in the United States were much more on the minds of these people than their own problems with Japan.

These developing countries are highly dependent on continued open trade in order to realize their goals for growth and industrialization. If the trade conflicts that are now attracting so much attention in the United States can be contained, then their goals may be met. Japan plays

61

a key role in this effort in two ways. First, it is a central focus in American frustration and must continue to liberalize its market to keep that frustration under control. Second, despite the current mild tone of criticism from the developing countries, more active liberalization efforts would enable them to increase their exports of manufactured goods to Japan as part of their development strategies.

Rapid economic development in the region has a nice intellectual appeal to it: Americans often like to support the general principle of rising incomes in other countries but then pursue protectionism out of fear that open trade policies to benefit these nations will destroy local jobs. Not only is that perception wrong in a broad economic view, but a strong argument can be made that liberal trade is in the strategic interest of the United States. Growth may well have contributed to the relative political stability in the region. All of these nations face certain problems, but in all cases economic growth has helped to subdue those problems. Unlike some developing countries, like Iran, where modern economic growth has brought changes that conflict with basic religious beliefs, the societies of Northeast Asia have been quite adaptable to rapid growth. In the three Northeast Asian NICs, rapid growth may have made their incomplete democracies more acceptable to the public. Therefore, a rise in protectionism stemming from American frustration over its trade ties with Japan and other countries in the region could slow economic growth and bring greater political instability.

The preceding pages have also pointed out that the large role of Japan in the region has by no means precluded the United States. In terms of trade and investment, the U.S. presence in most cases is equally strong and has shown little indication of diminishing. The rapid expansion of the economies of the region has permitted an increase in involvement for both Japan and the United States. Given the desire expressed in most of the countries to maintain some balance in their relations, or to avoid overdependence on any single trading partner, little change in this situation is likely. Put more bluntly, the fears sometimes expressed in the United States that a rupture in U.S.-Japan economic ties could lead to the formation of a "co-prosperity sphere" in Asia, with Japan at the center and excluding the United States, are silly. For both political and economic reasons, that eventuality is virtually unthinkable.

None of the above comments applies to Mongolia, North Korea and the Soviet Union. They have chosen virtually to isolate themselves from the rapidly expanding ties that have characterized the rest of the region, but their presence raises serious questions. On the one hand, their integration into the regional trade and investment ties bring economic gain to all parties, exemplified by the recent shift in China's external economic policies. On the other hand, such a move would be very ambiguous from a political standpoint. Would greater involvement of the Soviet

Union, for example, lead to decreased tension and make it a more responsible member of the world community? Or would the Soviet Union focus on using those ties to further its geopolitical goals, including an attempt to pry Japan away from its close relationship with the United States? Should Japan encourage closer ties with the Soviet Union in hopes of the former outcome, or should it react with great caution and suspicion out of fear of the latter? Past Soviet behavior suggests that its motives should not be viewed favorably, but this is at least a question that ought to be asked and explored.

China, on the other hand, has proven to be a positive factor. Its decision to pursue closer economic ties with the West has clearly led to a lessening of tensions in the region. Problems have not disappeared (especially the knotty question of Taiwan), but the knowledge that external economic ties are essential to its development goals has made China a more responsible member of the world community.

If the nations of Northeast Asia are to continue to grow and develop, then Japan must deal with two critical issues. First, it must be willing to adopt macroeconomic policies that shift its own growth away from dependence on exports toward domestic demand. The large Japanese trade surpluses and U.S. trade deficits that emerged in the first half of the 1980s are not sustainable either economically or politically in the long run. Both Japan and the United States must address this problem and continue the progress that began with the efforts to alter exchange rates in the fall of 1985.

Second, Japan must continue to lower barriers to its markets in order to contain criticism from abroad. Should Japan fail to do so, the result could well be a serious protectionist outburst by the United States which would necessarily spill over to the countries of the region. Both Japan and the United States bear the responsibility for managing their bilateral relationship, but the critical element will be Japan's willingness to continue the progress toward liberal trade.

If Japan, in conjunction with the United States, can appropriately manage its macroeconomic and trade policies, then the prospects for the region remain bright. But success in dealing with these problems is far from assured.

Suggested Reading

Bergsten, C. Fred and William R. Cline, *The United States-Japan Economic Problem*, Washington: Institute of International Economics, 1985.

Johnson, Chalmers, *MITI and the Japanese Miracle*, Stanford: Stanford University Press, 1982.

Lee, Chae-Jin, *The New Economic Diplomacy*, Stanford: Hoover Institution, 1984.

Lee, Chong-Sik, *Japan and Korea: The Political Dimension*, Stanford: Hoover Institution, 1985.

Lim, Linda Y.C., "Rising Trade Tensions: Asian Perspectives", in *Asian Issues 1985*, New York: The Asia Society, and Lanham, MD: University Press of America, 1986.

Lincoln, Edward J., *Japan's Industrial Policies*, Washington: Japan Economic Institute of America, April 1984.

Nakamura, Takafusa, *The Postwar Japanese Economy*, Tokyo: University of Tokyo Press, 1981.

Okimoto, Daniel I., ed., *Japan's Economy: Coping with Change in the International Environment*, Boulder: Westview Press, 1982.

Patrick, Hugh and Henry Rosovsky, *Asia's New Giant — How the Japanese Economy Works*, Washington: Brookings Institution, 1976.

Scalapino, Robert A., *Major Power Relations in Northeast Asia*, New York: The Asia Society, and Lanham, MD: University Press of America, 1986.

About the Author

Edward J. Lincoln has been a research associate in the Foreign Policy Studies Program at the Brookings Institution since 1984. He specializes on the Japanese economy and has a forthcoming book dealing with economic change in Japan since 1973. He also teaches about Japan at the Johns Hopkins School of Advanced International Studies. Prior to taking up his current position, Dr. Lincoln was Vice President of the Japan Economic Institute. He received his Ph.D. in economics at Yale University in 1978 and his undergraduate degree from Amherst College.